THE ULTIMATE

TEDDY BEAR
BOOK

THE ULTIMATE

TEDDY BEAR BOOK

PAULINE COCKRILL

Photography by
ROLAND KEMP

BOOKS U.K. LTD.
WALLSEND, ENGLAND.

A DORLING KINDERSLEY BOOK

Important Notice
Quotation marks indicate that a bear's name
was given by an owner

Art Editor
Vicki James

Editors
Susie Behar
Lynne Williams

Senior Art Editor
Gill Della Casa

Senior Editor
Mary-Clare Jerram

Production Controller
Rosalind Priestley

First published in Great Britain in 1988 by Dorling Kindersley Limited, London.
This 1993 edition produced exclusively for Books UK Ltd.

Copyright © 1991
Dorling Kindersley Limited, London
Text copyright © 1991 Pauline Cockrill

A CIP catalogue record for this book is available from the British Library

ISBN 187 161 225X

Computer Page Make-up by The Cooling Brown Partnership, Great Britain
Text Film Output by Creative Input, Great Britain
Reproduced by Colourscan, Singapore
Printed and Bound by Arnoldo Mondadori Editore, Italy

CONTENTS

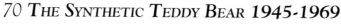

❖ INTRODUCTION ❖

Who would have thought that a craze nearly 90 years old would still be as popular today as it was in the beginning. How strange that an animal so ferocious in the wild has inspired the creation of such a soft and cuddly creature, a powerful emotive symbol of childhood, or of love between two people. The teddy bear, who began life as a mascot for the American president, Theodore Roosevelt, is now universally accepted as a child's first playmate and confidante. Today he features in millions of books, songs, comic strips, and films; he is used in children's therapy, and is the subject of "arctophily", a new hobby. (The word "arctophily" is derived from the Greek words "arctos", which means bear and "philos", which means love.)

TEDDY BEAR COLLECTIONS
The contents of a teddy bear collection varies according to the owner's taste, space and, of course, resources. Some people go to the extent of collecting anything that is somehow connected to teddy bears – even biscuit wrappers and postage stamps – while other collectors are more selective, eagerly searching out the older, top of the range bears, such as Steiff, Bing, Chad Valley, or Merrythought. Some concentrate solely on replicas, or examples made by modern teddy bear artists. A few arctophiles devote themselves with mission-like zeal to saving abandoned teddy bears from an uncertain fate, collecting out of love, and not necessarily for investment.

PERSONAL APPEAL
Teddy bears seem to have an unusual quality quite unlike other collectables. It is not long before most new acquisitions are given personalities, christened, and often clothed. Some bears are even presented with a ready-made past life. I have seen the most unlikely people talking to these inanimate objects. It is also true to say that the bears that fetch the highest prices are those that not only hail from well documented factories, but also have character.

WORLD-WIDE RECOGNITION
Teddy bear collecting has become so popular that some arctophiles have opened their collections to the public. Around the world, museums have recognized the great importance of the teddy bear. In 1983, in Lyon, France, an exhibition celebrated his 80th birthday. In 1984 and 1985, two German museums housed a "Teddy Bear and Company" exhibition, focusing on the history of the Steiff firm.

△ **First Friend**
A photograph, dating from 1905, illustrating the role of the teddy bear as a child's earliest and dearest companion, and confidante.

△ **Record Breaker**
Bunny Campione of Sotheby's, London, holding the Steiff bear "Happy" (see p.45). In 1989 this bear was auctioned for a record-breaking sum of £55,000 ($86,000).

△ **On all Fours**
Before the advent of the teddy bear, bears appeared on all fours, like this early Steiff.

▷ **Overbearing Bear**
The teddy bear's "larger than life" personality is captured in this old photograph.

THE MUSEUM OF CHILDHOOD

In 1984, I joined the curatorial staff of the Bethnal Green Museum of Childhood, a branch of London's Victoria and Albert Museum. I became a professional arctophile, quite by accident. An art historian by training, the endless stream of teddy bear enquiries seemed to find their way to my desk. Before long, I was receiving letters addressed to "the lady who loves teddy bears". I began to build up the Museum's collection of teddy bears. Many people came with their teddy bears to make sure that they approved of their old companion's final resting place. One teddy bear, in particular, was never forgotten by his elderly, former owner. He was sent a birthday card each year until his owner's death. "Little Tommy Tittlemouse" as he was called, was made as long ago as 1908. Though now completely bald, he lives on, staring out through the display case with beady, black eyes.

△ Bear Behind
Several picture postcard designs, from the first two decades of this century, make this risqué allusion.

▽ Rare Bear
Peter, made in 1925 by Gebrüder Süssenguth (see p.44), is rare and valuable.

STARTING A COLLECTION

How do you start collecting teddy bears? Before you actually buy a bear, it is a good idea to visit museums, shops, and antique fairs that deal exclusively with teddy bears. Browse through pre-sale catalogues or, if possible, attend preview days for sales devoted to teddy bears and other toys, at the major auction houses, such as Sotheby's, Christie's, or Phillips. Talk to as many experts as possible, and look through books like this one. *The Ultimate Teddy Bear Book* is designed with both the experienced and the first-time buyer in mind. Its catalogue pages give a front view and a side view of the bear, and point out significant details about the bear's features. It will soon become clear to even the first-time buyer that no two bears are the same – each has his or her own identity.

△ British Bear
Early British bears, like this one from the 1930s, are now prized.

◁ Happy Families
Paul and Rosemary Volpp with their three most precious possessions, the Steiff bears, "Bo", "Happy", and "Dearheart". The Volpps have an astounding 4,000 teddy bears housed at their home in California.

△ Pocket Size
These three 1920s Schuco bears are pocket-size.

TEDDY PARADE

Before World War I, teddy bears were bear-like, with pointed muzzles, humped backs, and long limbs. They were made of mohair plush in realistic colours, with felt pads on their feet and paws, and boot button eyes. At first, the principal manufacturer was the German company, Steiff, although Britain developed a thriving soft toy industry in the 1920s and 1930s. British bears were different from their European cousins, with flatter faces, shorter, straighter limbs, and eventually, no humpback. By the late 1940s, many bears were made of synthetic fibres, in less realistic colours, and they were filled with kapok instead of the traditional wood-wool stuffing. The shape of the teddy bear changed dramatically – a fatter, unjointed bear was emerging.

NEW BEARS, NEW MATERIALS

By 1964, bears were made entirely of synthetic materials, and the first, fully machine-washable bear was manufactured. However, the 1980s saw a revival of the traditional teddy bear for the new market of teddy bear collectors. A cottage industry developed making collectors' bears with natural materials, but in compliance with modern safety standards.

▷ **c.1905, German**
This Steiff bear, with its realistic bear-like shape and colour, is typical of its time.

▽ **c.1918, British**
A British version of the Steiff. It has shorter limbs, a long thin body, and a pointed muzzle projecting from his forehead.

▷ **c.1955, British**
A typical post-war bear with a large head, wide forehead, plastic eyes, stumpy limbs, pads made from Rexine, and wood-wool stuffing.

▷ **c.1964, British**
The first machine-washable bear made by Wendy Boston.

▽ **1950s, British**
A mohair plush bear with velveteen paws, plastic eyes, and bells in his ears.

▽ **1960s, Australian**
This tiny, unjointed teddy was manufactured by the firm, Jakas.

▽ **1921, German**
A later Steiff with slightly shorter and plumper limbs, and glass eyes instead of the early bears' boot buttons.

▽ **1930s, British**
These three bears are typical British examples of their time. They have short limbs, flat faces, and velveteen and woven cotton fabric instead of felt, for foot and paw pads.

▽ **1940s, British**
A Chiltern musical bear made from artificial silk/rayon plush. After 1930 this material was available in a variety of colours.

▽ **1940s, British**
Like many wartime bears, this one is made of sheepskin with leather pads.

▽ **1970s, American**
An unjointed bear manufactured with man-made materials by America's famous Knickerbocker Toy Co.. The parts were sewn together in Korea.

▽ **1988, American**
The American company, Applause, made this modern teddy out of synthetic plush stuffed with polyester wadding.

▽ **1987-8, German**
Teddy Rose is one of a limited edition of 10,000. He is a replica of a Steiff bear that was originally made in 1925.

▽ **1986, British**
A bear made by the family firm, Canterbury Bears.

▽ **1987, British**
Brian's Bear was made for the teddy bear shop, Asquiths. He is a fine example of a collectors' bear.

BEAR FEATURES

The design of the detailed features on a teddy bear – his eyes, his nose, his mouth, and his claws – has changed over the years. In conjunction with the overall shape, and the materials used in the construction of his body, the eyes, nose, mouth and claws can help you determine the date and provenance of a teddy bear, especially if, as is so often the case, no trademark exists.

EYES

Small, wooden boot button

Large, wooden boot button

Boot button on red felt

Small metal button

Clear glass, painted back

Eyes were held on wire shanks or hooks

NOSE

Hand-stitched in black

Moulded gutta-percha

Noses were usually hand-stitched with black or brown thread. An early natural plastic, called gutta-percha, was used on some bears, notably the rare metal-rodded 1904/5 Steiff.

MOUTH

Stitched, wide smile

The mouths of most bears during this period were the traditional, inverted V-shape: a single stitch on either side of a central, vertical stitch. A few bears, like the Columbia Laughing Bear, however, had open mouths revealing a row of teeth.

CLAWS

Four stitches to pad edge

Claws were usually indicated with black or brown thread: four stitches stretched from the edge of the pad across the plush.

Old and New Bears
(left) A Steiff bear dating from the early 1900s, sits next to a Steiff bear dating from the 1980s (right).

EYES
Eyes are probably the best indicators of age, although you should be wary of replacements. It can be difficult distinguishing glass from plastic: if you place your lip on an eye, glass will feel colder, and harder than plastic.

NOSE
Throughout history, teddy noses have been stitched with thread. The more unusual celluloid, tin, and leather noses often date from before World War II; moulded rubber or plastic noses appear on post-1950s bears.

MOUTH
The mouths on the vast majority of bears are suggested with black or brown stitching that forms an inverted V-shape. Variations on this theme give the different bears their individual expressions.

CLAWS
Stitching – in a variety of styles – is the most common way of indicating claws on a teddy's feet and paws. Some of the more unusual bears have claws moulded on their rubber or wooden pads.

1914–1944 | 1945–1969 | 1970–1990

Bulbous, opaque glass | *Rolling glass set in socket* | *Enamelled metal button*

Clear glass, painted back | *Amber and black glass* | *Blue and black glass*

Bulbous, brown glass | *Glass inside rubber socket* | *Safe, plastic screw-in*

From around 1955, the plastic screw-in eye was used by most bear manufacturers. The screw-in eye was considered much safer for children, than the eyes on wire shanks or hooks that were used previously.

Amber plastic | *Replica boot button* | *Replica metal button*

Manufacturers are now required by law to use safe, plastic, lock-in eyes for children's toys. Glass eyes and plastic replicas of traditional boot buttons are used for bears aimed at the collectors' market.

Vertical stitching (Steiff) | *Painted composition* | *Curled leather*

Vertical stitching (Merrythought) | *Vertical stitching* | Hand-stitched noses are still the most popular. The style of the stitching could vary according to the manufacturer.

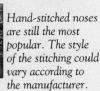

Painted tin | *Pink stitch across* | *Wide, rectangular, stitched*

Narrow, stitched | *Moulded rubber* | Moulded and plastic noses were used during this period.

Realistic, moulded plastic | *Stylized, bulbous plastic*

Safe, plastic, lock-in noses are common on children's teddies; bears made for the collector's market, however, usually had hand-stitched noses.

Stitched, wide, smiling | *One stitch* | *Double stitch*

Open, felt lining | *Open, teeth, moving tongue* | *Open, felt lining, tongue*

 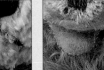

Traditional inverted V | *Open, felt lining* | *Hinged jaw, felt lining*

Stitched, wide, smiling | Manufacturers experimented with open and moving mouths, but hand-stitching continued to be the most popular means of indicating a bear's mouth.

Open, painted felt tongue. | *Single stitch*

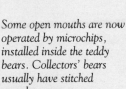 

Some open mouths are now operated by microchips, installed inside the teddy bears. Collectors' bears usually have stitched mouths.

Stitches across pad | *Stitch across plush and pad* | *Stitch across plush and pad*

 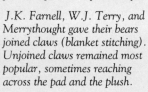

Blanket stitch | J.K. Farnell, W.J. Terry, and Merrythought gave their bears joined claws (blanket stitching). Unjoined claws remained most popular, sometimes reaching across the pad and the plush.

Moulded rubber with toes | *Stitches across plush and pads* | *Shaggy plush conceals claws*

Carved, wooden | *Stitches across pads* | *Stitches across plush*

Stitches in the traditional style, across the plush, the pads, or plush and pads, are still used for indicating claws. There are variations, however. Bears designed by Robert Raikes have claws carved into their wooden foot and paw pads.

❧ THE TEDDY IS BORN ❧

We can thank the 26th President of the United States, Theodore, or Teddy, Roosevelt for giving the teddy bear his name. In November 1902, this popular family man took a four-day break from politics to attend a bear hunt in Mississippi. The President was unlucky, and his only chance of a kill was a bear cornered and tied to a tree. He refused to shoot it. The incident was illustrated in the Washington Post by the political cartoonist, Clifford K. Berryman. Through Berryman, the little bear came to symbolize the President and featured in many of the artist's subsequent cartoons. Within a year, the cartoon bear had been transformed into a toy for children – the teddy bear.

A PRESIDENT'S MASCOT

Before the introduction of the teddy bear, the burgeoning toy industry of the 1880s had used the bear as a subject for automatons. These clockwork bears, which could dance, drink, or smoke, were very popular. Many originated from French manufacturers, such as Descamps, and Martin. In Germany, more realistic soft toy bears that stood on all fours and sometimes moved on wheels were made. There is no doubt, however, that it was as a mascot for President Roosevelt that the teddy bear proper came into being. A year after Berryman's cartoon, two Russian emigrés, Morris and Rose Michtom, transformed the cartoon bear into a jointed, plush teddy bear. The Michtoms sold their stock of bears to the wholesalers, Butler Bros., and founded the highly successful toy manufacturers, The Ideal Novelty and Toy Co..

△ **Drinking Bear**
An early clockwork drinking bear.

△ **Cartoon**
Berryman's original cartoon, depicting Teddy Roosevelt.

STEIFF ORIGINS

At the same time, jointed plush bears were being developed in Germany, by a family business headed by Margarete Steiff. Having contracted polio and been wheelchair bound since a child, she had become an expert seamstress, making children's clothes. In 1880 she formed a mail order company making soft toys and other items. The first was a pincushion elephant, an animal that was to appear on Steiff's first trademark. At first, the Steiff bears were unsuccessful, until the Leipzig Fair in March 1903, when Hermann Berg, a toy buyer for the New York department store, George Borgfeldt and Co., bought 3,000 teddy bears. In 1905, the Steiff bear was legally protected by the famous "button in ear" trademark. He was so popular that the factory was forced to expand three times between 1903 and 1908. During this period, known as the *Barenjahre* (Bear Years), the number of teddy bears produced annually rose dramatically from 12,000 to about 975,000 – a phenomenal figure

△ **Founder**
Margarete Steiff.

△ **Theodore Roosevelt**
The original "Teddy", greatly loved by the American people.

◁ **Steiff Factory**
In 1905, the Steiff factory at Giengen am Brenz employed about 2,000 workers to make teddy bears.

△ **Teddy B and Teddy G**
Seymour Eaton's bears appeared in 20 American newspapers.

△ **Cut-outs**
Printed cotton cut-out bear, patented in 1905 by the British Dean's Rag Book Co..

△ **Trademarks**
The trademark of the British United Manufacturing Co., and Aetna Toy Animal Co..

never since repeated. The teddy bear's popularity was boosted by the introduction of Seymour Eaton's *Roosevelt Bears*. These rhyming tales originally appeared in American Sunday supplements from 1905, and were then published in four books between 1906 and 1907. The tales started with *The Roosevelt Bears, their Travels and Adventures* which inspired many novelties such as mugs, spoons, and books. By about 1907, Teddy's Bear was universally known as the teddy bear, and had become well established in the home.

GERMANY AND THE UNITED STATES

Soft toy manufacturers, both in Europe and the United States, increased in numbers in an attempt to keep up with growing demand. In Germany, the centre of the toy industry, many doll and toy firms, such as Gebrüder Bing, Fleischmann, and Bloedel, turned their attention to making teddy bears. In 1913, stimulated by the teddy bear phenomenon, Max, Arthur, and Adelheid Hermann started making teddy bears at their father's wooden toy factory. In the United States, the demand for teddy bears was met similarly. Toy firms like the American Doll and Toy Manufacturing Co. began producing mohair plush bears from about 1906. Other manufacturers, such as Hahn & Amberg, makers of leather goods, also turned to teddy bears. Some companies, such as Aetna and Bruin, were short-lived, but all tried to equal the imported Steiff bears, as revealed in advertisements by Hecla and the Miller Manufacturing Co..

BRITISH TEDDIES

In Britain, the teddy bear enjoyed considerable success. He first appeared in 1909 in a children's story, *The Tale of Teddy Bright Eyes*. It is possible that the toy's success was also fuelled by the country's own "Teddy", King Edward VII. The majority of teddy bears originated from the Steiff factory in Germany, but a handful of soft toy manufacturers established in the late nineteenth century, principally the London based companies of William J. Terry (est. 1890), the British United Toy Manufacturing Co. (est. 1894), and J. K. Farnell (est.1897), made some bears. In 1903, Henry Samuel Dean established Dean's Rag Book Co., near London's Fleet Street. Along with the rag books "for children who wear their food and eat their clothes", they produced various printed cotton toys, including teddy bears. Their first plush bears were not introduced until just before World War I.

△ **Model Bears**
Teddy Bears soon became important photographic accessories.

▽ **Terryer Toys**
A dog was the trademark of British soft toy manufacturer, William J. Terry.

△ **Heirloom**
Probably one of the original Ideal bears, this bear was presented to Roosevelt's grandson. It now lives in Washington D.C., in the Smithsonian Institute.

BEAR NECESSITIES

With few exceptions, early teddy bears were made from natural materials: a mohair plush fabric, wood-wool stuffing, boot button eyes, felt paws and embroidered details. After experimentation, a joint system, giving bears a mobile head and limbs, was perfected, and a squeaker or growler mechanism became an essential requirement.

Wooden boot buttons

EYES
Wooden boot button eyes with metal loops on the back were sewn into the bear's face. Some British firms preferred black metal buttons. Miniature bears were given small, glass bead eyes on wire shanks.

White mohair plush

Golden mohair plush

Glass bead eye

Glass eye on wire shank

Pairs of glass eyes joined by lengths of wire

FUR FABRICS
Soft toy animals had been made from real fur, but with the introduction of the teddy bear, mohair plush, a cheaper imitation fabric, was invented. Soft, silky, and dirt-resistant, it is woven from the fleece of the angora goat.

Brown mohair plush

1905 STEIFF
This bear is typical of the period, with his brown mohair plush, and boot button eyes.

BURLAP
A few early bears were made from burlap, a brown, coarsely woven material. Produced from jute, a fibre found in tree bark, it was imported from the Indian subcontinent.

Burlap

Felt scrap

Cardboard discs

Small pin

Metal washer

Cotter pin

BOARD JOINTS
One cardboard disc is attached to the limb, the other is part of the main body. Both discs rotated on a small pin, inserted through a metal washer. A felt scrap acted as a buffer between the discs.

Cotton thread

Metal and cardboard discs

SEAM THREAD
After the bear had been stuffed, a very strong thread was used for hand-sewing the final openings of the body, head and tops of limbs.

METAL JOINTS
Sometimes, metal discs were used with cardboard discs to give the jointing system greater strength. The discs rotated on a cotter pin, (with double prongs that splayed out).

MOULDED NOSE
Some early bears had moulded noses that were made from gutta-percha – a natural plastic.

Gutta-percha

Embroidery silks

Cotton thread

Felt

HAND-STITCHED DETAILS
Thick embroidery silk created countless noses, mouths, and claws. The individual parts of the bear were machine-stitched with cotton thread to match the mohair plush.

FELT PADS
Paw and foot pads on early bears were made of felt. The most common colours were beige and cream, although black was sometimes used for black bears. (Coloured felt was sometimes used to reinforce the pads.)

TILT GROWLER
In 1908, tilt growlers were introduced. Contained in a cardboard tube, a lead weight opened or closed the bellows when the bear was tilted, forcing air over the reed, and so creating a growl.

Lead weight

PUNCH GROWLER
One of the earliest voice boxes consisted of a bag of oilcloth. By punching or squeezing the bear's stomach, containing the bag, the rush of air caused the reed inside to vibrate.

Bellows made with wood and oilcloth

Oilcloth bag

Gauze speaker

Cardboard container holding tilt growler

WOOD-WOOL STUFFING
Also known as straw stuffing, wood-wool is made from long, fine-quality wood shavings, previously used as a packing material for delicate objects, such as china. Cork granules, another packing material, provided an alternative stuffing for printed cloth bears.

Wood-wool

Reed contained within tubing

REED
The same type of reed was used in growlers and squeakers.

KAPOK PACKING
Kapok is a protective, silky fibre that comes from the seed pod of a tropical tree. Steiff used it as a packing around voice boxes; Farnell found it good for filling the tips of paws.

Oilcloth strip binding

Coiled spring

Kapok

SQUEAKER
Squeakers were used before tilt growlers. When the bear's stomach was squeezed, air vibrated the reed that was fixed to the underside of one of the pieces of wood or card.

BEAR APPAREL

The clothes a child chooses for his or her teddy bear can provide an insight into the relationship between the two of them. A child's instinct to treat a bear like a human, and dress it, presented manufacturers with an opportunity they could not afford to miss. The teddy's doll-like, jointed body made him ideal for outfits of every conceivable form, and as soon as 1906, teddy bear manufacturers had set about clothing him. Steiff produced a series of dressed bears, which included Basa and Basi in sailor suits or dresses, and Batro, who wore a knitted suit and cap.

BEARS FOR THE BOYS
In the United States, the teddy bear was marketed as the boy's toy, as an alternative to his sister's doll, and so commercially made clothes often reflected his masculine character: there were suits for policemen, firemen, and sailor bears, and "Rough Rider" outfits – the uniform of Roosevelt's U.S. volunteer cavalry – were also popular. Steiff, D.W. Shoyer and Co., and Kahn and Mossbacher, all produced suits with the names of Teddy B and Teddy G (see pp.12-13) embroidered on the chest or sleeve.

Δ **Top Hat**
An Edwardian traveller's sample, found in an antique market, makes an obvious accessory for an aristocratic bear.

Δ **The Casual Look**
A 1906 Steiff bear wearing a double-breasted knitted suit with brass buttons.

IMPROVISED OUTFITS

Garments designed especially for teddy bears were expensive in the early 1900s. So naturally, children and parents often made the clothes themselves, using patterns found in such magazines as the American *Ladies Home Journal*, *The Delineator*, or *The Woman's Home Companion*. Home-made outfits, based on contemporary clothing, were common, and the cast-offs of dolls or babies were also useful. University students dressed their bears in knitted suits, consisting of a sweater, trousers, and a cap, all in the appropriate college colours. As few of the teddy clothes made in the early 1900s have survived today, collectors tend to seek out Edwardian baby clothing, such as bonnets and gowns, and period accessories: bags, watches, and jewellery. Dressing teddy bears is very enjoyable, but there are also some less obvious advantages from this hobby: clothes protect a bear from dust and light, and also help disguise the fact that he or she may be missing a limb or two.

△ *Scholarly Bear*
The addition of accessories, preferably contemporary, adds greatly to a bear's personality. This 1905 Steiff, with mortar board and satchel, would have appealed enormously to school children and students.

△ *Edwardian Chic*
An Edwardian child's bonnet and bloomers, made from broderie anglaise and lace-trimmed cotton, evokes a bygone era.

◁ *The Cattley Toys*
Now in London's Bethnal Green Museum of Childhood, this collection dates from about 1906. The teddy bears originally belonged to five children of the Cattley family, who created all their bear outfits themselves. They made full sets of underwear, using remnants of broderie anglaise, velvet, and lace.

▷ *Nautical Teddy*
A 1911 bear proudly shows off a World War I naval uniform, and an unusual hand-stitched shirt.

BEAR MEMORABILIA

The craze for the teddy bear, and all things related, is not a recent phenomenon. As early as 1907, the teddy bear's popularity was reaching great heights, and soft toy makers competed to produce bears with additional novelty appeal, such as teddies with reversible heads. Other factories turned their hands to producing metal, china, wood, rubber, and celluloid bears. In the United States, the teddy bear's influence was so pervasive that the bear appeared on postcards, advertising material, and song sheets. Over 400 copyrights for song titles, using the words "teddy" or "teddy bear", were registered between 1907 and 1911.

NOVELTY BEARS

Almost from the beginning, teddy bears that could squeak or growl were made, but it was not long before manufacturers attempted to produce something a little different. In 1907 the Self-whistling Bear, which whistled when turned upside down, and the Musical Bear, with a turn handle musical box, were produced by Strauss, the "toy king" of New York. From New York, too, came the Columbia Teddy Bear Manufacturers' Laughing Bear, with open jaws of pointed teeth, and the Electric Bright Eye Bear, patented on 19 February, 1907, by the Fast Black Skirt Co.. The Electric Bright Eye Bear had red or white eyes that lit up when its right paw was squeezed. Various moving teddy bears were also made, some with no clockwork mechanism, such as Mrs Gillespie's Tumbling Bear of New York. In 1911, in Germany, a fierce legal battle ensued between two manufacturers, Steiff and Bing, over the patent of two similar somersaulting clockwork bears. In 1913, Steiff made a bear, known as a Record Bear, which could be pulled along on a four-wheeled metal chassis, with a squeaker on the rear axle.

△ **Teething Ring**
The hollow silver teddy bear, with ball bearings, and a bone teething ring, dates from 1910.

△ **Teddy Buttons**
Mohair plush coats with teddy bear brass buttons were popular with American children around 1907.

△ **Bisque Bear**
An unglazed porcelain bear with jointed limbs.

△ **Song Sheet**
A detail from the front cover of the sheet music for The Teddy Bear's Frolic, published in London, in 1910.

▽ **Bear In A Box**
Miniature bears were popular from the outset. This example, with his own trunk, was originally bought at a London market stall.

FROM RATTLES TO JUMPING JACKS

Teddy bears featured on nursery items, such as babies' ceramic bowls, throughout this period. American silver feeders and teaspoons were embossed with teddy bears climbing the handle or engraved on the bowl. Rattles designed as fur fabric sticks, with a teddy bear head at each end, were made, although particularly collectable (and possibly more useful) are the silver cast rattles and teething rings, produced both in the United States and Britain. One of the "bearskin" – mohair plush – coats for young children, made from black, brown, white, or blue mohair, with teddy bear embossed brass buttons is a rare find. Another sought after item is the Steiff hot water bottle of 1909. This was made in the shape of a traditional, jointed bear with a tin canister inside, accessible through a laced-up central front seam. Teddy bear-inspired board, card, and parlour games abounded, as did teddy ABC blocks, chime toys, money boxes, jumping jacks, tea sets, and teddy bear jewellery.

△ English Plate
This 1912 child's plate shows a popular design.

▽ Clothing
The muff shown below, as worn by its original, young owner. The photograph dates from between about 1905 and 1910.

◁ Acrobatic Bear
Similar to the Steiff tumbling bear (see p.40) this rare, Bing clockwork bear, dating from about 1910, performs acrobatic feats when his arms are rotated.

△ Teddy Bear Muff
Several manufacturers, including Steiff, made children's muffs in the shape of fat teddy bears.

❧ "Mrs Robinson" ❧

1904 IDEAL NOVELTY & TOY CO.

"Mrs Robinson" is said to be one of the early teddy prototypes, manufactured by the Ideal Novelty & Toy Co., the first company to produce teddy bears in the United States. In 1938, they became the highly successful Ideal Toy Corporation, who were taken over by CBS Inc. in 1982 when, sadly, teddy bears were discontinued.

EARS
Ideal bears usually have much rounder ears than those of "Mrs Robinson".

EYES
Like so many of the teddy bears made before World War I, "Mrs Robinson" has black, wooden, boot button eyes, sewn just inside the seam of her face.

Long, protruding muzzle

CLAWS
Each foot and paw has four claws, embroidered in a double thickness of light brown thread.

FEET
Her feet are neither as long nor as narrow as those belonging to her Steiff cousins. The oval pads are covered with beige felt, reinforced with card.

The pads of early Ideal bears were narrow at the toe ends

Bear profile A large, rounded head, gentle sloping forehead, and peculiarly accentuated hump on the back, make "Mrs Robinson's" profile distinct from her American contemporaries'.

NOSE
The triangular nose of rust-coloured broadcloth, secured with stitching of the same colour, is the work of a repairer. The original would have been hand-stitched in the same brown thread as her mouth and claws.

ARMS
"Mrs Robinson's" long, tapering arms are curved at the paw ends, much like those of the early Steiff bears.

Beige mohair plush

• BEAR ESSENTIALS •

HT: 42cm (17in)

FUR: beige-coloured, mohair plush
EYES: small, black, wooden, boot buttons
EARS: large, placed wide apart and low
MUZZLE: long, protruding, and pointed

NOSE: broadcloth, triangular, rust
ARMS: long, curved; beige, felt pads; claws
FEET: large, oval; beige, felt pads; claws
STUFFING: wood-wool throughout bear

DISTINGUISHING FEATURES: The unique, upwardly pointing hump projecting out from "Mrs Robinson's" back sets her apart from contemporary, American bears.

❧ "Eddie" ❧

c.1903-1905 STEIFF

The blank, nickel-plated button in "Eddie's" left ear represents the prototype of Steiff's now famous trademark. Originally the idea of Richard Steiff's younger brother, Franz, the button was stamped for a brief period with the elephant logo. The word "Steiff" was introduced on 13 May, 1905, the year the button was patented.

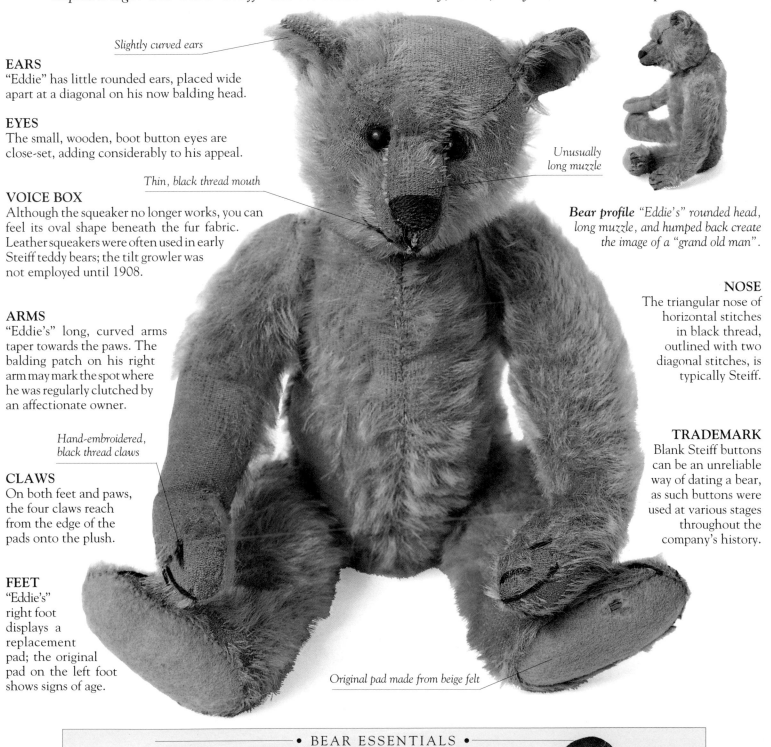

Slightly curved ears

EARS
"Eddie" has little rounded ears, placed wide apart at a diagonal on his now balding head.

EYES
The small, wooden, boot button eyes are close-set, adding considerably to his appeal.

Thin, black thread mouth

VOICE BOX
Although the squeaker no longer works, you can feel its oval shape beneath the fur fabric. Leather squeakers were often used in early Steiff teddy bears; the tilt growler was not employed until 1908.

ARMS
"Eddie's" long, curved arms taper towards the paws. The balding patch on his right arm may mark the spot where he was regularly clutched by an affectionate owner.

Hand-embroidered, black thread claws

CLAWS
On both feet and paws, the four claws reach from the edge of the pads onto the plush.

FEET
"Eddie's" right foot displays a replacement pad; the original pad on the left foot shows signs of age.

Unusually long muzzle

Bear profile *"Eddie's" rounded head, long muzzle, and humped back create the image of a "grand old man".*

NOSE
The triangular nose of horizontal stitches in black thread, outlined with two diagonal stitches, is typically Steiff.

TRADEMARK
Blank Steiff buttons can be an unreliable way of dating a bear, as such buttons were used at various stages throughout the company's history.

Original pad made from beige felt

• BEAR ESSENTIALS •

HT: 33cm (13in)

FUR: beige-coloured, worn, mohair plush
EYES: small, wooden, boot buttons, close set
EARS: small, rounded, set wide apart
MUZZLE: thin and long, protruding

NOSE: hand-embroidered, triangular, black
ARMS: long, curved; beige, felt pads; claws
FEET: large, narrow; beige pads, claws
STUFFING: wood-wool throughout bear

Blank button

Trademark

❧ "Oscar" ❧
1904-1905 STEIFF

After the 1903 Leipzig Fair, Richard Steiff created two new bears, both with gutta-percha noses. The Bär 35 PB still had thread joints, but Bär 28 PB, of which "Oscar" is an example, had metal rods – a system patented in 1905. Bär 28 PB was available only for a brief period and is therefore rare.

Horizontal, ear-to-ear seam

EARS
His ears are made from two semi-circles of plush material, sewn into seams on both the sides and the top of his head.

EYES
Black-painted, wooden boot buttons are sewn just on the outer side of each of the bear's two face seams.

VOICE BOX
These early, metal-jointed bears were mute, as growlers were not fitted into Steiff bears until about 1905.

JOINTS
"Oscar" has a pair of metal rods, with card discs at the ends, running horizontally through his body. These rods join his legs and arms. Another metal rod extends vertically from the centre of the upper rod, connecting his body and head.

Worn pads show wood-wool stuffing

FEET
Like so many bears of this early period, his feet are large and pointed.

Mouth was probably an inverted "V"

Bear profile The side view clearly shows his prominent, humped back and long, curved arms. Also visible is his closely clipped, almost fox-like muzzle, with its well-defined, moulded nose.

NOSE
His life-like nose is made of gutta-percha, an early type of natural plastic, which was also used for making practical, domestic items such as buckets.

CLAWS
Black thread is used to embroider the five claws. After 1905, Steiff bears were given only four claws.

Long, curved paws

STUFFING
"Oscar" is filled with wood-wool throughout. As in all Steiff bears, the final opening is the centre seam at the front. This is hand-sewn, using strong thread.

• BEAR ESSENTIALS •

HT: 40cm (16in)

FUR: beige, mohair plush, some clipped short
EYES: small, black, wooden boot buttons
EARS: small, unstuffed, placed wide apart
MUZZLE: long, tapering, plush clipped short

NOSE: gutta-percha, life-like, oval, black
ARMS: long, tapered; beige, felt pads; claws
FEET: long, pointed; beige, felt pads; claws
STUFFING: wood-wool throughout bear

Trademark

Elephant button

❧ "Friend Petz" ❧
1903-1905 STEIFF

Still known as "Bärle" in the catalogues, and not as yet as the teddy bear, by 1905 Steiff's creation had become less like a bear and more like a bear-doll. It now had a refined, swivel joint system, a voice box, and rounder features. Various sizes and colours were produced, and the famous trademark "button in ear" was patented.

EARS
This bear is particularly unusual because of his ears. They are large and flat, and sit rather low down on the sides of his head.

EYES
Like most of the early bears, boot buttons are used as eyes.

Clipped mohair plush muzzle

VOICE BOX
Sadly, in the older bear, the voice box tends not to work any more. Prodding or shaking the poor creature is the only way of checking if he has one in his torso.

Long, tapering arms

FEET
"Friend Petz" has long, narrow feet – and shapely ankles – typical of this period. The red, felt reinforcement, commonly used in early Steiff bears, can be seen poking through the felt pads.

Beige, felt pads repaired with stitching

Bear profile A side view of "Friend Petz" shows the chief features of these early, solid and rounded bears – humpback, pointed muzzle, long, curved limbs, and large feet.

NOSE AND MOUTH
Both of these have been hand-embroidered in a beige thread, using vertical stitches.

Beige, shaggy mohair plush

PAWS
His spoon-like paws curve upwards, and have beige, felt pads.

CLAWS
The claws are outlined in the same beige thread that is used for the mouth and nose.

• BEAR ESSENTIALS •

HT: 65cm (25in)

FUR: beige, somewhat shaggy, mohair plush
EYES: large, black, boot buttons, close-set
EARS: large, flat, unstuffed, on side of head
MUZZLE: long, tapering, short clipped plush

NOSE: hand-embroidered, heart-shaped, beige
ARMS: long, curved; beige, felt pads; claws
FEET: long, narrow; beige, felt pads; claws
STUFFING: wood-wool throughout bear

TRADEMARK: Originally this beige, shaggy bear would have had a Steiff button and label in its ear for easy identification, but sadly, it is missing from "Friend Petz".

❧ "Maximilian" ❧

1905 STEIFF

Named "Maximilian" by an early owner, this Steiff shares many of the characteristics of "Friend Petz" (see p.23). However, by 1905, the classic Steiff bear shape was becoming less naturalistic, and "Maximilian" has a smaller hump and more rounded muzzle than his opposite number.

EARS
Compared with those of earlier bears, his ears have changed noticeably, both in shape and in the angle at which they are positioned on his head.

Black, wooden boot button eyes

HEAD
"Maximilian" has a central seam running down his muzzle, a common feature in early Steiffs, although rare in teddy bears generally. It exists because the size of the bear's pattern allowed only six complete heads to be cut out of each length of mohair. The seventh head was, therefore, always cut in half, resulting in a seam in the bear's face.

Bear profile *His muzzle and hump seem to be less prominent than those of "Friend Petz", resembling the more doll-related toy that the teddy bear was soon to become.*

NOSE AND MOUTH
Both were recently replaced in black wool, although a similar black thread would have been used originally.

PADS
All of his pads have been replaced with new, dark brown felt in an attempt to combat excess wear and tear.

Green cravat adds a touch of formality

FUR
The curly, cinnamon, mohair plush is in mint condition.

The original felt would have been lighter

Thin ankles and narrow feet

• BEAR ESSENTIALS •

HT: 56cm (22in)

FUR: cinnamon-coloured, curly mohair plush
EYES: rounded, black, wooden boot buttons
EARS: small, unstuffed, placed high on head
MUZZLE: pronounced but blunt, fur clipped

NOSE: hand-embroidered, rectangular, black
ARMS: long; brown, felt pads; no claws
FEET: narrow; brown, felt pads; no claws
STUFFING: wood-wool throughout bear

Raised lettering

Trademark

❧ "Blissful" ❧

1907 BRUIN MANUFACTURING CO.

Despite importing thousands of teddy bears from Germany, by 1907 the United States had established numerous firms to keep up with the demand for the Roosevelt-inspired mascots. Few early American bears can be positively identified. However, "Blissful" carries the label of the short-lived Bruin Manufacturing Co..

EARS
Like Ideal's "Mrs Robinson" (*see p.20*), his ears are set well apart, above his very wide forehead and partly down the sides of his head. However, his ears are smaller.

EYES
Like so many teddy bears of this early period, "Blissful" has black, wooden, boot button eyes.

VOICE BOX
There is a worn patch on his stomach where his squeaker has been repeatedly pushed.

Golden mohair plush

STUFFING
Originally stuffed with wood-wool, it seems that at some time in the bear's life, a softer filling, perhaps kapok, was also added.

Woven label stitched across right foot

FEET
"Blissful" has large feet which are quite long, with pads of beige-coloured felt.

Bear profile "Blissful" has a typical, early American bear body. His triangular-shaped muzzle extends directly from his forehead, and he has a traditional humpback.

NOSE AND MOUTH
The mouth and rectangular nose are represented by stitches of black thread.

ARMS
Wide shoulders run into long arms, tapering to thin, curved paws with beige, felt pads.

CLAWS
This bear has four short claws on each foot and paw pad.

Black thread claws sewn to edges of pads

• BEAR ESSENTIALS •

HT: 33cm (13in)

FUR: golden-coloured, long, mohair plush
EYES: small, black boot buttons in face seams
EARS: small, slightly cupped, wide apart
MUZZLE: triangular, extends from forehead

NOSE: hand-embroidered, rectangular, black
ARMS: long, curved; beige, felt pads; claws
FEET: large; beige, felt pads; claws
STUFFING: wood-wool, kapok restuffing

Trademark

❧ "Still Hope" ❧

1907 AETNA TOY ANIMAL CO.

"Still Hope" was manufactured by one of the many American firms set up during this period. Its products also included jointed rabbits and monkeys. He was named after an ancestor of his present owners, who was scalped by native Americans and left for dead, but then recovered and lived until she was 110.

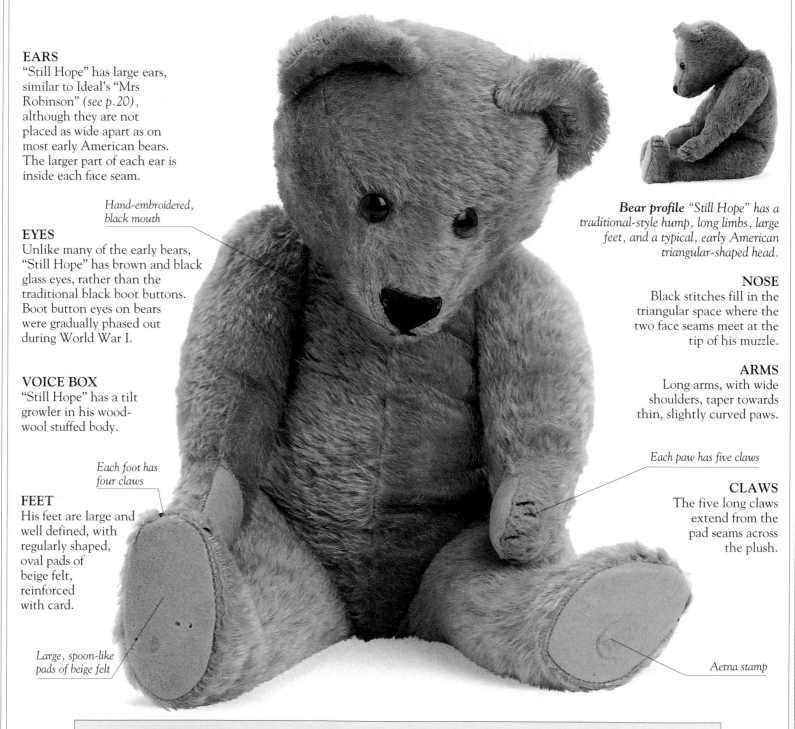

EARS
"Still Hope" has large ears, similar to Ideal's "Mrs Robinson" (see p.20), although they are not placed as wide apart as on most early American bears. The larger part of each ear is inside each face seam.

Hand-embroidered, black mouth

EYES
Unlike many of the early bears, "Still Hope" has brown and black glass eyes, rather than the traditional black boot buttons. Boot button eyes on bears were gradually phased out during World War I.

VOICE BOX
"Still Hope" has a tilt growler in his wood-wool stuffed body.

Each foot has four claws

FEET
His feet are large and well defined, with regularly shaped, oval pads of beige felt, reinforced with card.

Large, spoon-like pads of beige felt

Bear profile *"Still Hope" has a traditional-style hump, long limbs, large feet, and a typical, early American triangular-shaped head.*

NOSE
Black stitches fill in the triangular space where the two face seams meet at the tip of his muzzle.

ARMS
Long arms, with wide shoulders, taper towards thin, slightly curved paws.

Each paw has five claws

CLAWS
The five long claws extend from the pad seams across the plush.

Aetna stamp

• BEAR ESSENTIALS •

HT: 50cm (20in)

FUR: beige, somewhat worn, mohair plush
EYES: large, brown and black, glass, close-set
EARS: large, set into facial seams across head
MUZZLE: protruding, extension of forehead

NOSE: hand-embroidered, triangular, black
ARMS: long, curved; beige, felt pads; claws
FEET: large; beige, felt pads; claws
STUFFING: wood-wool throughout bear

TRADEMARK: An ink stamp bearing the company's trade name "Aetna", set in an oval black line, is imprinted onto the centre of the bear's left foot pad.

❧ "Wistful" ❧

1907 BRUIN MANUFACTURING CO.

Although unmarked, "Wistful" is thought to have been made in New York by Bruin, whose rivals in the city included Ideal, Aetna, the Harman Manufacturing Co., and the American Doll and Toy Manufacturing Co.. At first, mohair plush was imported from Europe, but soon the United States began to set up its own mills.

EARS
"Wistful" has small, rounded ears although, like Bruin's "Blissful" *(see p.25)*, they sit wide apart on his extensive forehead.

Edges of ears just caught into the face seams

EYES
Unlike "Blissful", "Wistful" has brown and black glass eyes, one of which is probably a replacement. They are sewn into the seams running from his ears to his nose.

Mouth curves upwards

FUR
His long, golden mohair plush was probably produced locally. Thousands of angora goats were kept to meet the growing demand for teddy bear fur. His muzzle is covered with the same mohair as his head and body.

Short black claws

FEET
His feet are large and slightly narrower than those of the other early American bears. They have long, beige, felt pads.

Bear profile "Wistful" has a face like a fox, with a sharp, triangular-shaped muzzle. His elongated body is typical of the early American bear.

Replacement glass eye

NOSE
The end of his muzzle is bound with vertical stitches of black thread that form a long, rectangular nose. This is the work of a repairer.

Well-worn muzzle

ARMS
"Wistful" has long and tapering arms which curve at the point where they merge into paws. The paws have large, beige, felt pads.

CLAWS
Five embroidered black claws are on both the feet and paws. The relatively short stitches extend only from the seam edges across the plush.

Beige, felt pads are well worn

• BEAR ESSENTIALS •

HT: 37cm (14in)

FUR: golden-coloured, long, mohair plush
EYES: small, brown with black pupils, glass
EARS: small, rounded, set wide apart in seams
MUZZLE: protruding, extension of forehead

NOSE: hand-embroidered, rectangular, black
ARMS: long, tapering; beige, felt pads; claws
FEET: large, narrow; beige, felt pads; claws
STUFFING: wood-wool throughout bear

DISTINGUISHING FEATURES: The unusual, long and rectangular nose of this golden bear differs from more common, square noses. The vertical stitching is repair work.

❧ "*Avalon*" ❧

c.1910 GEBRUDER BING

After 1905, the demand for teddy bears began to soar dramatically and, in response, the German manufacturers Gebrüder Bing produced their own version of a bear. The company had been making domestic tinware since 1865, and had turned to the production of enamelled and clockwork toys at the end of the nineteenth century.

EARS
Unlike most Steiff bears of the time, "Avalon's" ears sit quite far down his forehead.

Distinctly curved head

Round, rigid ears

EYES
The replacements are in keeping with the original black boot buttons.

NOSE AND MOUTH
The black vertical stitches representing the nose are original, but the mouth has been repaired using matching black thread.

CLAWS
"Avalon" still has four black thread claws on each foot. The claws on his paws, however, have become unstitched.

FEET
Beige felt pads are reinforced with thick card so that "Avalon" can stand upright.

Bear profile In shape, this Bing bear is noticeably rounder than his contemporaries. His legs and feet are stumpier than those on Steiff bears.

FUR
The curly mohair plush is in superb condition, although his clipped muzzle is a little worn in places.

Elegant, felt-covered paws

ARMS
The slightly curved arms are in the tradition of early bears.

• BEAR ESSENTIALS •

HT: 57cm (23in)

FUR: beige-coloured, curly, mohair plush
EYES: medium, black, plastic, boot buttons
EARS: small, round, high over face seams
MUZZLE: blunt, protruding, clipped mohair

NOSE: hand-embroidered, black thread
ARMS: long; beige, felt pads; claws
FEET: large, oval; beige, felt pads; claws
STUFFING: wood-wool throughout bear

TRADEMARK: Originally bears like "Avalon" would have had a metal arrow tag with GBN on the ear or a button on the body. Avalon has the metal arrow tag.

❧ "Bing Oh!" ☙

c.1911 GEBRUDER BING

In about 1909, Steiff took action to prevent Gebrüder Bing, then probably the largest toy manufacturer in the world, from using a button-in-ear trademark. A metal arrow temporarily replaced the Bing button, until Steiff granted the right for an underarm stud to be used, providing no reference was made to the word "button".

EARS
"Bing Oh!" has large, rounded ears. Set wide apart, they sit towards the back and down the sides of his head.

EYES
Traditional black boot buttons are used for eyes. They are sewn into the facial seams.

Clipped, plush muzzle

VOICE BOX
"Bing Oh!" has a tilt growler inside his wood-wool stuffed body.

TRADEMARK
A metal arrow under this bear's right arm was all that Steiff would allow its rival company to use. The word "button" remained the property of Steiff.

FEET
The very large feet have narrow, extremely long pads similar to those belonging to "Friend Petz" (see p.23) and "Maximilian" (see p.24), both early Steiff bears.

Bear profile *From this angle you can see the similarity between "Bing Oh!" and Steiff bears of the same period: the protruding muzzle, humped back, long limbs and large feet.*

NOSE AND MOUTH
The nose is hand embroidered with vertical stitches of black thread. His mouth is the traditional inverted V-shape with a few vertical stitches joining it to the nose.

ARMS
The long, tapering arms are curved at the paws – similar to those of Steiff bears.

Leather pads replace the original felt pads

Long, dark brown, mohair plush

• BEAR ESSENTIALS •

HT: 53cm (21in)

FUR: dark brown, long, mohair plush
EYES: medium, black, wooden, boot buttons
EARS: large, rounded, placed wide apart
MUZZLE: protruding, clipped mohair plush

NOSE: hand-embroidered, triangular, black
ARMS: curved; brown, leather pads; no claws
FEET: large; brown, leather pads; no claws
STUFFING: wood-wool throughout bear

Trademark

❧ "Miss Nightingale" ❧

1912 BRITISH

Although unmarked, this bear is known to have been made in Britain before World War I, dispelling the theory that all early bears are either German or American. A number of British firms manufactured soft toys from the late nineteenth century, using plush cloth produced in the towns of Huddersfield and Dewsbury.

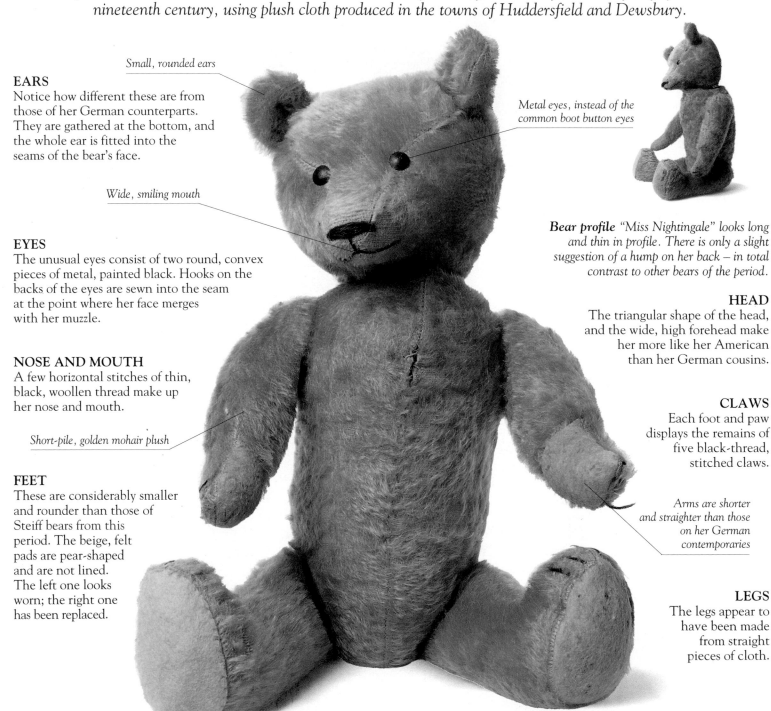

Small, rounded ears

EARS
Notice how different these are from those of her German counterparts. They are gathered at the bottom, and the whole ear is fitted into the seams of the bear's face.

Wide, smiling mouth

EYES
The unusual eyes consist of two round, convex pieces of metal, painted black. Hooks on the backs of the eyes are sewn into the seam at the point where her face merges with her muzzle.

NOSE AND MOUTH
A few horizontal stitches of thin, black, woollen thread make up her nose and mouth.

Short-pile, golden mohair plush

FEET
These are considerably smaller and rounder than those of Steiff bears from this period. The beige, felt pads are pear-shaped and are not lined. The left one looks worn; the right one has been replaced.

Metal eyes, instead of the common boot button eyes

Bear profile *"Miss Nightingale" looks long and thin in profile. There is only a slight suggestion of a hump on her back – in total contrast to other bears of the period.*

HEAD
The triangular shape of the head, and the wide, high forehead make her more like her American than her German cousins.

CLAWS
Each foot and paw displays the remains of five black-thread, stitched claws.

Arms are shorter and straighter than those on her German contemporaries

LEGS
The legs appear to have been made from straight pieces of cloth.

• BEAR ESSENTIALS •

HT: 47cm (19in)

FUR: golden, short-pile, mohair plush
EYES: small, black, metal buttons
EARS: small, rounded, gathered at base
MUZZLE: pointed, thin, down-turned

NOSE: hand-embroidered, rectangular, black
ARMS: tapering; beige, felt pads; claws
FEET: short; beige, felt pads; claws
STUFFING: wood-wool throughout bear

DISTINGUISHING FEATURES: This straight, thin bear has a long, narrow-hipped, wide-chested body, and relatively short arms, compared with her contemporaries.

❧ "Marmaduke" ❧

c.1913 WILLIAM J. TERRY

This bear is said to have been made by William J. Terry, one of the forerunners of the British soft toy industry. A photograph exists of similar teddies made by this east London-based firm, showing them for sale in London's first department store, Whiteleys, in the West End.

EARS
His semi-circular ears are wider than the small, pert ones of the 1912 British bear (*see p.30*), but are similarly perched in each "corner" of his triangular-shaped head.

Large eyes give an appealing, wide-eyed expression

EYES
The backs of his clear glass eyes are painted an unusual shade of pink. Toy catalogue photographs of this time show glass eyes in William J. Terry's soft toys.

VOICE BOX
A prod in the tummy suggests he contains a growler, although it no longer works. It was probably the tilt variety (*see pp.14-15*).

FEET AND PAWS
Two layers of a now discoloured, and slightly damaged, thin woven fabric represent foot and paw pads. This suggests that they are replacement pads, or else the remains of the original lining.

Long, egg-shaped feet

Bear profile *The straight, tubular body, and peculiar Mr Punch-like hunchback, make this bear unique.*

NOSE AND MOUTH
Stitches in a green, woollen thread make up the nose, and the mouth is formed using the same thin thread. This is an unusual colour, so the stitches are probably the work of a repairer.

Long, silky, blond mohair plush

CLAWS
The green wool defining the claws may be repair work – the original stitching was probably black.

Long, curved, tapering arms

• BEAR ESSENTIALS •

HT: 40cm (16in)

FUR: blond, long and silky, mohair plush
EYES: large, clear, glass, pink-painted backs
EARS: small half circles, set high on head
MUZZLE: pointed with blunt tip, clipped

NOSE: hand-sewn, rectangular, green wool
ARMS: long; discoloured, woven pads; claws
FEET: large; discoloured, woven pads; claws
STUFFING: wood-wool throughout bear

TRADEMARK: This bear does not have a trademark. William J. Terry bears often had card swing tags reading: "Terryer Toys"; "Marmaduke" may once have had one.

❧ "Bobby" ❧

1908 STEIFF

In 1908 Steiff introduced the Maulkorb-bär. A special characteristic of this bear was his leather "muzzle" and leading rein, a feature inspired by dancing bears that performed in town squares of central Europe. Manufactured in brown or white, the bear was available in ten sizes. Steiff made a replica of the white muzzled bear in 1990.

EYES
"Bobby" has the small, wooden, boot button eyes commonly used by manufacturers, especially Steiff, throughout this period.

VOICE BOX
Although now no longer working, "Bobby" has a squeaker mechanism. It was around this time that Steiff began to use the first tilt growlers inside their bears.

ACCESSORIES
"Bobby's" "muzzle" is made of leather, which has darkened with age. It is held together with round studs, which resemble the blank, metal buttons used as trademarks on early Steiff bears. The "muzzle" is fastened at the back with a buckle, and has a leading rein attached.

TRADEMARK
"Bobby" has a 1905-1950 Steiff button, bearing the name of the company.

FEET
His large feet have beige, replacement, felt pads. They are close in colour to the original.

The small, rounded ears are positioned well apart

Bear profile "Bobby's" accentuated limbs, his leather muzzle and its fastenings, and the leading rein, now broken, are clear from this angle.

Typical inverted V-shaped mouth hidden by "muzzle"

NOSE
His triangular nose is embroidered in black thread. The stitching is identical to that on "Eddie's" nose *(see p.21)*.

ARMS
The long and tapering arms have curved paws with replacement, beige, felt pads.

CLAWS
The four claws of black thread extend across the plush section of each of the paws.

Light brown mohair plush

• BEAR ESSENTIALS •

HT: 26cm (10in)

FUR: light brown-coloured, mohair plush
EYES: small, black, wooden boot buttons
EARS: small, rounded, positioned wide apart
MUZZLE: long, protruding; leather "muzzle"

NOSE: hand-embroidered, triangular, black
ARMS: long, curved; beige, felt pads; claws
FEET: large; beige, felt pads; claws
STUFFING: wood-wool throughout bear

Raised lettering

Trademark

⚘ "Othello" ⚘

1912 STEIFF

"Othello" belongs to a batch of black bears produced by Steiff for the British market. Coming in five sizes, they were manufactured in either short or long mohair plush. Long mohair plush bears, like "Othello", are the rarest as only 494 of them were made. Steiff made one other black bear in 1907; it had red claws and a gutta-percha nose.

EARS
"Othello" has large ears, set wide apart. Like the ears of many early Steiff bears, they are sewn into the seams of his face.

Orange felt makes eyes more prominent

EYES
Each black, boot button eye is set on a circle of orange felt. This is a unique feature, as the 1907 black Steiff bear had no backing for his boot button eyes.

TRADEMARK
"Othello" has the famous Steiff "button in ear" trademark used from 1905 to 1950.

FEET
His large feet have long, narrow pads of beige felt. There are no claws stitched onto his feet and paws because the black thread normally used to match the nose would not have shown up against the bear's dark fur.

Feet in mint condition

Bear profile The long limbs, protruding muzzle, and unusual felt and boot button eyes, are clearly defined in profile.

NOSE AND MOUTH
The hand-embroidered nose is large and rectangular. It consists of vertical, black thread stitches. The stitched mouth is an inverted V-shape.

ARMS
"Othello's" arms are long, tapering, and curved in the traditional manner, with pads of undamaged beige felt.

Long, black mohair plush

• BEAR ESSENTIALS •

HT: 48cm (19in)

FUR: black, long, shaggy, mohair plush
EYES: medium, black, boot buttons on felt
EARS: large, set wide apart into face seams
MUZZLE: blunt, protruding, clipped

NOSE: hand-embroidered, rectangular, black
ARMS: curved; beige, felt pads; no claws
FEET: large; long, beige, felt pads; no claws
STUFFING: wood-wool throughout bear

Raised lettering

Trademark

❧ THE TEDDY BEAR EXPLOSION ❧

*W*orld War I was to have a serious effect on the toy industry, which had been a German monopoly since the 19th century. With borders closed and bans on German imports in many European countries, German manufacturers found business very difficult. The way was open for the soft toy industry to develop elsewhere. The French company, Thiennot, manufactured one of their first teddy bears in 1919. In Britain, several soft toy firms were established during World War I, utilizing the Yorkshire woven mohair plush fabric, much of which had been previously exported to Germany. By the 1920s, Britain was producing some of the finest teddy bears in the world.

BRITISH MANUFACTURERS

1914 signalled a halt to German-made teddy bears. Many factories were given over to making items for the war effort. Both partners of the newly formed Nuremberg-based Schreyer and Co. were drafted into military service, as were the three Steiff directors. In Britain, however, a number of toy factories were established, some specifically for making teddy bears. William Henry Jones, originally a representative for doll manufacturers in Germany, found himself jobless as a result of the war so he turned to designing teddy bears. Other new companies dating from 1914 included the East London Federation Toy Factory, established by Sylvia Pankhurst.

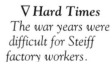

▽ **Homemade**
A teddy made in a British home.

TEDDY TRADENAMES

Many of these firms had registered tradenames, such as the South Wales Manufacturing Co.'s Madingland or Joseph Burman's Zoo Toy Co.'s Fondle Toys. These were rarely attached to the bear in any permanent form, creating problems for today's collectors. The Mr Teddy card swing tag of the Liverpool-based Messrs Gray & Nicholls is really only known through photographs in trade catalogues. Catalogues such as the *British Games and Toys* or *The Toy Trader* and the *American Playthings* help greatly with research. By the 1930s, the leaders of the British soft toy industry were all in existence, each with patented trademarks often in the form of more permanent buttons or embroidered labels, a boon for today's collector. Dean's A1 and Farnell's Alpha bears were well established. By 1920, Chad Valley's Wrekin

△ **Photographic Evidence**
Photographs of bears that still live on with their original owners, are popular with collectors today.

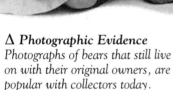

△ **German Trademark**
The trademark used by Bernhard Hermann in the 1920s.

▽ **New Company**
The Teddy Toy Co. was founded in London in 1914.

MANUFACTURERS OF **ALL-BRITISH SOFT TOYS**

▽ **Hard Times**
The war years were difficult for Steiff factory workers.

△ Chest Tag
Ges. gesch on this trademark means "legally protected".

soft toy factory in Wellington, Shropshire, had been opened, and H.G. Stone & Co. were producing their Chiltern range of teddy bears from their Chesham factory. A decade later, Merrythought had joined the ranks, the result of a partnership between W.G. Holmes and G.H. Laxton. 1937 saw the creation of another important teddy bear manufacturer, Pedigree Soft Toys, as well as the voluntary liquidation of W.H. Jones. This was the beginning of the end of many small businesses, who were unable to cope with increasing competition and economic depression.

NEW MATERIALS

The use of new materials changed the shape and feel of the teddy bear. Kapok was greatly preferred by British firms, not only for its softer, lighter and more hygienic qualities, but also because it could be bought cheaply from countries within the British Empire. Teddy bears with coats of artificial silk plush, woven from fibres consisting of reconstituted cellulose from woody plants, were introduced, often dyed in a range of colours. As early as 1919, the Wholesale Toy Co. was offering a pink teddy bear.

WORLD WAR II

The coming of World War II had a dramatic effect on the manufacture of the teddy bear. Hitler's rise to power in 1933 left many German toy companies and export houses in disarray. In Britain, Farnell's factory was bombed during the London blitz, while output in many companies was gradually turned over to essential supplies. Dean's made life jackets, and Merrythought made helmet linings, hot-water bottle covers, and gas mask bags. Some companies, like Chad Valley were allowed to produce a limited toy quota. Rather touchingly, their 1942 advertisement featured a teddy bear with the words, "Though his fur is shorter and his stuffing less silky than in times of peace, the same care goes into his production ...".

△ Collector in the Making
Plummy is photographed here with his young owner who was later to collect and restore teddy bears for a living.

▽ Wartime Evacuees
Teddy bears were a great source of comfort to the children who were evacuated during World War II.

△ Mascot
The pioneer British airwoman, Amy Johnson (1903-1941) with her teddy bear mascot.

▷ A1 Toys
The trademark for Dean's Rag Book Co. in the 1920s.

△ H.G. Stone's Trademark
"Chiltern" refers to the site of the factory.

△ Postcards
Teddy bear postcards have always been popular with collectors.

BEAR NECESSITIES

As the teddy bear evolved, his limbs grew shorter, his body fatter, and his muzzle less pronounced. Synthetic plush fabrics, such as rayon and nylon, were introduced, glass eyes became the norm, and kapok stuffing was used for the entire body, producing a more cuddly toy. During both World Wars, no mohair plush was available and kapok was in short supply, so substitutes had to be found.

Glass eyes with wire shanks

Boot buttons

Clear glass eye

Glass eyes on wire hooks

Wired glass eyes

EYES
Boot buttons were used until the early 1920s, although Steiff went over to glass completely in 1921: glass eyes were held on short wire hooks or long wire shanks.

c.1930 BRITISH
This British bear has glass eyes, velveteen pads and kapok stuffing – new developments in teddy design – but still has mohair plush.

WOOL AND THREAD
During World War II, rationing of raw materials kept teddy bears in short supply, while parents resorted to knitting soft toys from unravelled wool.

1930s woven silk mohair plush

FABRIC
Woven mohair plush continued to be popular, but the invention of man-made fibres revolutionized the soft toy industry. In the 1920s artificial silk plush (rayon plush) was made; the first completely synthetic fibre, nylon, was invented in 1938.

Woven mohair plush

Woven mohair and synthetic plush

Woven nylon and acrylic plush

Sheepskin

Artificial silk plush (rayon plush)

JOINTS
The combination of metal and cardboard discs inside the jointing system of some bears remained unchanged (*see p.14*).

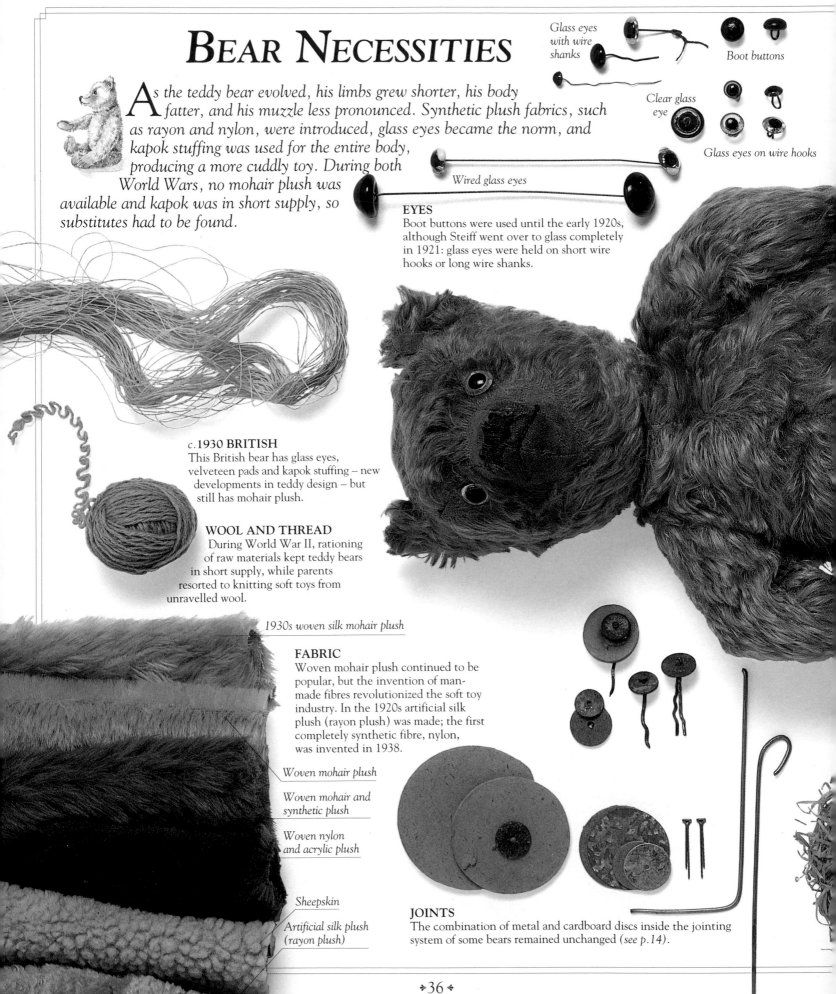

Embroidery thread

Thread for machine-stitching

Cardboard

Felt

Velveteen

Woven cotton

Rexine

PAW AND FOOT PADS
Cardboard was used in the earlier period for reinforcing the feet, but it was especially typical of 1920s and 1930s teddy bears. Claws (as well as noses and mouths) were sewn with embroidery thread.

FELT AND FABRIC PADS
Throughout this period, pads were made from felt, although other materials were used as well. Velveteen – a short pile cotton fabric – cotton and brushed cotton fabrics, and Rexine, the trade name for a kind of treated muslin or oilcloth used by English manufacturers from about 1930, were all popular.

Interior of tilt growler

Squeaker

SQUEAKER
The oval card and oilcloth squeakers were still used in teddy bears throughout this period.

1920s TILT GROWLER
Tilt growlers with weighted, hinged bellows, were used up until the 1920s, although their cardboard canisters became slightly more sophisticated – the lids were made from perforated card instead of gauze.

Tilt growler showing perforated, card lid

Tilt growler mechanism

Porcelain weight

Oilcloth bellows

1930s TILT GROWLER
In the new tilt growler of the 1930s, a porcelain weight operated the bellows, forcing air over the reed, and through a waxed paper membrane.

Kapok

wood-wool

Sub and wood-wool

STUFFING
Although wood-wool was still used, kapok soon became popular for stuffing the entire bear, following its success as a filling in life-jackets during World War I. Its hollow, silky fibres attracted neither vermin, insects, nor bacteria, making it hygienic, light, and cuddly. After 1939, kapok was in short supply, so a substitute called sub, art wool, or flock, was developed from the waste material of the textile mills.

Sub

Inside of music box

Music box lid

Brahms' Lullaby
1849

Musical box

MUSICAL BOXES
By the 1930s, many bears contained musical boxes operated on the Swiss comb and toothed-cylinder principle: once wound up, a canister turned, letting the tuned teeth of a comb strike the pins and produce a tune. Brahms' *Lullaby* and *The Teddy Bears' Picnic* were common tunes.

BEAR APPAREL

With the introduction of newspaper comic strips, and cartoon characters in the cinema, soft toy manufacturers turned from producing naturalistic animals to caricatured cats, dogs, rabbits, and teddy bears; the outfits on some of these soft toys were as humorous as their expressions. During the 1920s and 1930s, teddy bears were made with their clothes and bodies all-in-one, so that they could not be undressed. One popular source of teddy outfits were the knitting patterns that appeared in the ever-increasing numbers of women's magazines. During the two World Wars, teddy bears became patriotic mascots and were dressed in military uniforms.

TEDDY CLOWNS

During the 1920s and 1930s, there was a particular demand for dressed bears in the United States. Steiff produced a number of bears in costume especially for the American market. An example was their white, blond or dark brown plush Teddybu. He was made in four sizes from 1925 to 1927, and wore a felt, three-buttoned waistcoat. Their Teddy Clown of 1926-8 came in eleven sizes in pink, gold, or brown-tipped mohair plush, complete with ruff and pierrot hat. Bears in clown outfits had been available in the United States since about 1907, and owe their popularity to the appearance of teddy clowns in Seymour Eaton's Roosevelt Bear books. Clown suits often formed part of the complete teddy bear trousseaus available in the United States during the 1930s. These trousseaus consisted of a trunk of clothes, including, for example, a red Indian, a cowboy, a Tyrolean, and a ski outfit.

△ **Going Dutch**
In the 1930s Dutch trousers were popular.

◁ **Trilbies**
During this period, some teddy bears were dressed in travellers' samples, such as trilbies.

△ **Pageboy**
This Chiltern teddy bear's pageboy uniform is all-in-one with the body. Made in the 1930s, it was also available in pink plush.

▷ **Home-made Outfit**
The outfit and scarlet tam o'shanter were lovingly knitted by the bear's seven-year-old English owner in 1944. Many other wartime teds were given similar clothes.

▷ **Gas Mask**
A gas mask for a teddy bear made from tin and oilcloth.

WARTIME TEDS

The outbreak of World War I inspired a number of patriotic mascots, including the teddy bear. It became the fashion to dress teddy bears in uniforms identical to that of a father, husband, brother, or sweetheart who had gone to the front. Many people made their own uniforms – some are still worn by the soldier and sailor bears on show at the Pollock's Toy Museum, and the Bethnal Green Museum of Childhood, respectively, in London. Teddy bears dressed in Russian clothes were particulary popular. In 1915, for example, the London Toy Co. designed Ivan, the Russian Tommy.

ALLY BEARS

A few uniforms were made commercially. The most famous are worn by the Ally Bears, a charming collection of teddy bears dressed in the various uniforms of the allied forces. They were manufactured by a London firm, Harwin and Co., from 1915. The Ally Bears were designed by the director's daughter, Dorothy Harwin, and they include a British sailor and admiral, a Red Cross nurse, and various soldiers, including a Scot, wearing a kilt, sporran, and spats, and an Australian wearing a turned-up, wide-brimmed hat, tilted across one ear. Ally Bears are rarely found intact today, although you can see one at the Museum of Childhood, Sudbury Hall, England.

△ *1930s Bare Bears*
Bears designed to be clothed, were made with no hair on their bodies.

△ *Regimental Dress*
During World War II, this 1905 Steiff bear found himself wearing the uniform of the Scottish regiment, the Black Watch.

▷ *Master Teddy*
This 1915 teddy with his typical "googly eyes" was produced by the Chiltern Toy Works of Chesham, later to become H.G. Stone & Co. Ltd..

BEAR MEMORABILIA

The years between the two World Wars saw a continuing demand for teddy bear novelties. Numerous clockwork bears were produced by the major manufacturers, although they are hard for collectors to identify, as they are often similar in subject, and many do not have trademarks. Miniature Schuco bears produced in various colours were very popular. Musical bears, dressed, for example, as clowns were made in the United States and Europe, and the teddy bear acquired his own theme tune when, in 1930, the British songwriter, Jimmy Kennedy added lyrics to the score, The Teddy Bears Picnic.

△ *Clockwork*
A 1915 Steiff bear that somersault

△ *Two-faced Bear*
A 1930s Schuco bear.

NEW TEDDY BEAR DESIGNS

The banning of the sale in Britain of German goods during World War I, and the subsequent rise of the British soft toy industry, resulted in the introduction of various innovations to the basic teddy bear design in Britain. In 1916, the British Doll and Novelty Co. made the teddy bear exerciser for children: the action of fully extending the bear's spring-loaded arms was considered beneficial to a child's muscles. In 1918, Messrs Isaacs and Co. made the Spring Leg Teddy Bear who had long legs and Wellington boots fitted with their patent "Isa" springs, which were activated when the child pulled at his leading rein. A series of kapok-stuffed, mohair plush toys called Bendy Bears were made by Deans in the early 1920s. Each had an internal metal framework that allowed the bear to be manipulated. H.G. Stone copied the Schuco style bears, with nodding heads. Their own Wagmee series was introduced in the late 1930s, and Steiff developed similar bears.

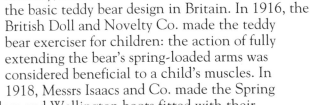

▽ *Compact Bear*
A compact made in the 1930s by Schuco. It had a mirror, a powder container, and a central stem to hold lipstick. Other Schuco bears were made to hold perfume.

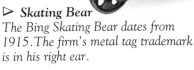

◁ *Two-tone Bear*
This bear's fur is dyed to make him resemble a clown. Two-tone bears were especially popular.

▷ *Skating Bear*
The Bing Skating Bear dates from 1915. The firm's metal tag trademark is in his right ear.

△ **1930s Record**
The Teddy Bears Picnic

CLOCKWORK BEARS

The clockwork bears of this period are probably the most interesting and, if in working order, they fetch high prices on today's market. Collectors should, especially, look out for Gebrüder Bing's Walking Bear of c.1915. It had a large key in its belly that operated its mechanism. Bing also produced tumbling bears, as did Steiff and Schuco. Bing and Schuco made skating bears that may have been inspired by Alice Teddy, a real bear that roller-skated in the United States before World War I. The Schuco Skating Bear wore a felt uniform and cap; his large metal feet had wheels attached to them. In the mid-1920s, Steiff made their Urteddy. This was similar to the earlier wheeled teddy *(see pp.18-19)*, but it also had a clockwork mechanism attached to the chassis. Other wheeled bears, such as Teddy Baby *(see p.49)* and Baby Bear, who lay appealingly on his back with bells on his paws, were produced. In the 1920s and 1930s, the teddy bear was developed as a container. Steiff was the first to do this with their unique teddy-shaped purses and tea cosies. In London, J. and A.J. Burman made their Teddy to-T, a teddy bear with an empty stomach that could be used as a small case.

◁ **Pill Box Hat**
This felt, pill box hat is slightly worn, although the leather strap is in good shape.

△ **Bag**
This Schuco bear still has a leather bag on a strap slung across his chest. It is unusual to find this particular Schuco bear with his accessories intact.

◁ **Bellhop Bear**
A Schuco bear dating from 1923. He is fully jointed and wears the smart felt livery of a hotel bellhop. The bear's tail operates his moving head. He also has a squeaker inside his chest. He is very rare, made more valuable by the fact that he is in mint condition and he retains his trademark.

△ **Gas Mask and Case**
A gas mask case with a plush teddy bear in felt clothing on its side. This was designed to comfort a British child during World War II.

❧ "Louise" ❧

1921 STEIFF

During World War I, the Steiff factory produced only war supplies, such as ammunition, aeroplane parts, and gas masks for horses. After the war, however, the introduction of the American conveyor belt system in 1921 improved efficiency, and the factory was soon on its feet again, producing bears like "Louise".

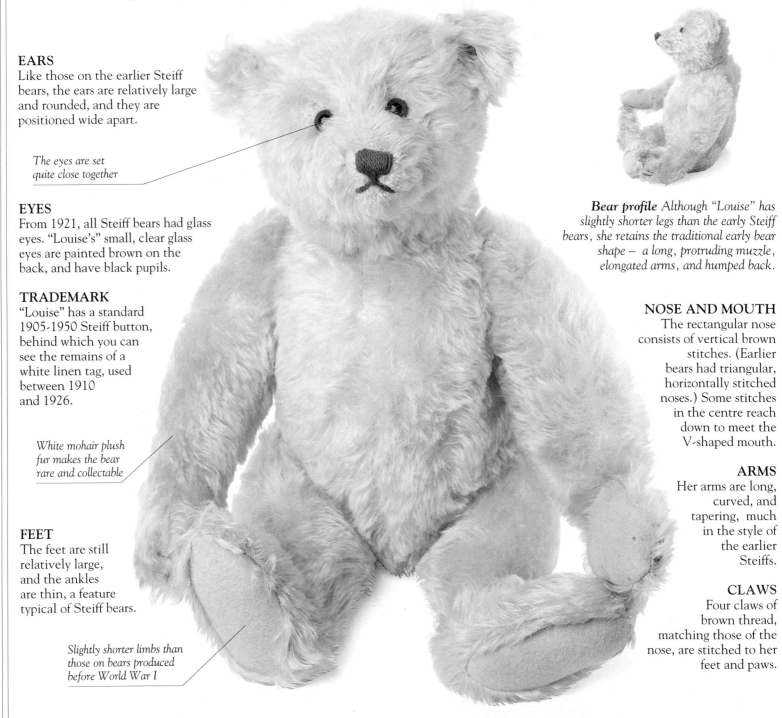

EARS
Like those on the earlier Steiff bears, the ears are relatively large and rounded, and they are positioned wide apart.

The eyes are set quite close together

EYES
From 1921, all Steiff bears had glass eyes. "Louise's" small, clear glass eyes are painted brown on the back, and have black pupils.

TRADEMARK
"Louise" has a standard 1905-1950 Steiff button, behind which you can see the remains of a white linen tag, used between 1910 and 1926.

White mohair plush fur makes the bear rare and collectable

FEET
The feet are still relatively large, and the ankles are thin, a feature typical of Steiff bears.

Slightly shorter limbs than those on bears produced before World War I

Bear profile *Although "Louise" has slightly shorter legs than the early Steiff bears, she retains the traditional early bear shape – a long, protruding muzzle, elongated arms, and humped back.*

NOSE AND MOUTH
The rectangular nose consists of vertical brown stitches. (Earlier bears had triangular, horizontally stitched noses.) Some stitches in the centre reach down to meet the V-shaped mouth.

ARMS
Her arms are long, curved, and tapering, much in the style of the earlier Steiffs.

CLAWS
Four claws of brown thread, matching those of the nose, are stitched to her feet and paws.

• BEAR ESSENTIALS •

HT: 39cm (15in)

FUR: white, shaggy, mohair plush
EYES: small, clear glass, brown-painted backs
EARS: large, rounded, placed wide apart
MUZZLE: slightly raised, protruding

NOSE: hand-embroidered, rectangular, brown
ARMS: long, curved; cream, felt pads; claws
FEET: large; long, cream, felt pads; claws
STUFFING: wood-wool and kapok mixture

STEIFF

Raised lettering

Trademark

❧ "Mr Fluffy" ❧

1923 CHAD VALLEY

This bear was manufactured at the Wrekin factory in Wellington, Shropshire, by the British toy company, Chad Valley. The firm began to specialize in soft toys in 1920. "Mr Fluffy" is one of their earliest teddy bears carrying the Aerolite trademark, an indication that kapok was used as a stuffing.

Large, flat ears on the sides of the head

EYES
His rich amber eyes with black pupils are made from glass, and are held on wire shanks. They are stitched into place.

VOICE BOX
The round, squeaker-type voice box, which can be felt at the front of the body, no longer works.

STUFFING
Aerolite is the trade name for the kapok stuffing used in bears of this period. While the limbs of this bear are filled with kapok, his head and body are probably a mixture of kapok and the more compact, wood-wool.

TRADEMARK
The small, metal button has an off-white celluloid centre, bearing the Aerolite trademark. The button, used by Chad Valley between 1923 and 1926, was intended to imitate Steiff's mark of excellence, without violating the patent.

Thick card reinforces the velveteen pads

FEET
The soles are more oval than those found on the feet of the earlier Steiffs.

Bear profile *The round, protruding forehead and prominent but blunt muzzle, the less accentuated humpback, and shorter limbs, all reveal the emergence of a new teddy bear shape.*

NOSE AND MOUTH
The triangular nose consists mainly of vertical stitches, with a few horizontal stitches along the top. Originally, the nose was black, but some of the outermost stitches have become discoloured with age. The inverted, V-shaped mouth curls upwards slightly to form an endearing smile.

Four black, stitched claws on each paw

FUR
A long-pile golden mohair was used for most of the bear – the mohair on his muzzle is clipped.

The arms are slightly shorter than those of the early bears

There are five claws on each foot

• BEAR ESSENTIALS •

HT: 40cm (16in)

FUR: golden, long, silky, mohair plush
EYES: medium, amber, glass, black pupils
EARS: large, flat, placed on side of head
MUZZLE: blunt, protruding, clipped plush

NOSE: hand-embroidered, triangular, black
ARMS: curved; large, velveteen pads; claws
FEET: large, oval, velveteen pads; claws
STUFFING: wood-wool and kapok mixture

Aerolite mark

Trademark

❧ Peter ❧

1925 GEBRUDER SUSSENGUTH

Peter was the novel creation of the Süssenguth factory in Neustadt-bei-Coburg, Germany, which had manufactured and exported dolls and toys since 1894. Few of these bears were sold at the time because, it is said, the bear's rolling eyes and bared teeth frightened children. Consequently, this bear is now rare.

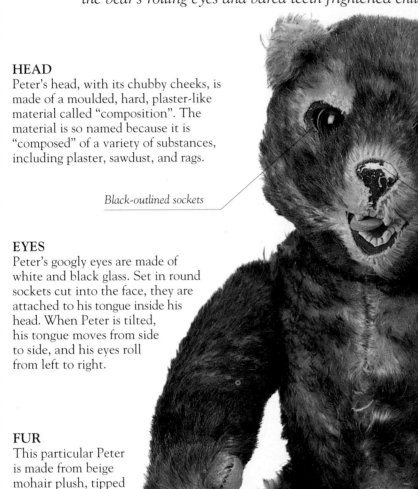

HEAD
Peter's head, with its chubby cheeks, is made of a moulded, hard, plaster-like material called "composition". The material is so named because it is "composed" of a variety of substances, including plaster, sawdust, and rags.

Black-outlined sockets

EYES
Peter's googly eyes are made of white and black glass. Set in round sockets cut into the face, they are attached to his tongue inside his head. When Peter is tilted, his tongue moves from side to side, and his eyes roll from left to right.

FUR
This particular Peter is made from beige mohair plush, tipped with dark brown. He was also produced in grey tipped with black, as well as gold plush. Bears made in gold plush are the most unusual.

STUFFING
While his body and limbs are stuffed with wood-wool, the moulded composition head is hollow.

Hollow head contains movable eyes and tongue

Bear profile *From the side, you can see Peter's long, straight back, and his open mouth with a moving, protruding tongue.*

White composition visible beneath peeling black paint

NOSE
The nose is moulded to portray two nostrils. It extends from beneath the plush, and is part of the hollow, composition head.

MOUTH
Peter's open mouth reveals moulded teeth, outlined in red paint. He even has two extended canines in the top jaw, and these are made from the same material as his head and nose. The movable tongue, a thin pointed piece of composition, is pale pink.

Notice the absence of claws on the feet

• BEAR ESSENTIALS •

HT: 35cm (14in)

FUR: brown-tipped, beige, dual mohair plush
EYES: large, white and black, glass, deep-set
EARS: small, round, set towards back of head
MUZZLE: pointed; open, moulded mouth

NOSE: moulded composition, square, black
ARMS: long; flesh-coloured, felt pads; no claws
FEET: long; flesh-coloured, felt pads; no claws
STUFFING: composition and wood-wool

TRADEMARK: A printed, round, card swing tag is often attached to the Peter's chest reading: "Peter Ges. Gesch. Nr 895257." It is legally protected.

❧ "Happy" ❧
1926 STEIFF

In 1989, "Happy" was sold at Sotheby's in London for £55,000 (US $86,350), and still holds the record for being the most expensive teddy bear bought at auction. The new owner presented "Happy" to his wife as a wedding anniversary present. The bear now lives in California.

EARS
The large, rounded ears are set wide apart, and sit on the sides, rather than the top, of her head. Their positioning is very similar to that on some of the earlier Steiff bears, like "Friend Petz" *(see p.23).*

Her large, brown glass eyes have black pupils

EYES
"Happy" has brown, glass eyes. She was possibly designed as a prototype for the Petsy bear registered in 1927. Petsy had brown or blue, glass eyes. The bears with blue eyes are more collectable.

VOICE BOX
"Happy" has a squeaker mechanism, although it no longer works.

FEET
Her large feet, with narrow pads, are pre-World War I style.

Bear profile Notice her long limbs, humped back, and large head with a protruding muzzle.

NOSE
Hand-embroidered in brown thread, her nose echoes the colour of the dual plush. It is large, heart-shaped, and consists of vertical stitches.

Long, tapering arms end in curved paws

FUR
Her attractive, dual mohair plush was extremely popular in the 1920s.

Large, spoon-like pads in the style of early German bears

• BEAR ESSENTIALS •

HT: 62cm (24in)

FUR: brown-tipped beige, dual mohair plush
EYES: large, brown, glass with black pupils
EARS: large, round, wide apart, side of head
MUZZLE: long, blunt, and protruding

NOSE : hand-embroidered, heart-shaped, brown
ARMS: long, tapering; beige, felt pads; claws
FEET: large, narrow; beige, felt pads; no claws
STUFFING: wood-wool throughout bear

Raised lettering

Trademark

❧ "Claus" ❧

1927 BERNHARD HERMANN

"Claus" is a product of the Gebrüder Hermann factory, founded by Bernhard Hermann around 1912. "Claus" was made in Sonneberg, then the centre of the toy-making industry. Steiff and Hermann bears can be difficult to tell apart, although the muzzle on a Hermann is often made from a different material to the rest of his body.

Slightly gathered ears

EARS
Two semi-circles of cloth form each ear. The back of the ear is made from the dual plush used for the rest of the body, while the front has the same short-piled mohair that covers the muzzle. The ears are placed centrally across the top of the two facial seams.

EYES
The bear's glass eyes are brown with black pupils.

Both the nose and mouth are embroidered with black thread

NOSE AND MOUTH
His nose is portrayed with horizontal stitches and the mouth has a gentle, upward curve.

STUFFING
The head, limbs, and body of this bear are all filled with wood-wool.

FEET
The clearly defined feet are quite small, and they have oval, cream felt pads.

Bear profile *"Claus" has a straighter back and less rounded head than the Steiff examples.*

ARMS
The arms are characteristic of those on early bears – long, curved, and slightly tapering, with pads of cream-coloured felt.

Black thread claws stitched onto the plush parts of the paws

FUR
The main body is made in dual-coloured, mohair plush: beige, tipped with rich cinnamon. This plush was a popular material in the 1920s. On the muzzle (and fronts of the ears) a short-piled, cream mohair plush is used.

• BEAR ESSENTIALS •

HT: 42cm (17in)

FUR: cinnamon-tipped beige, mohair plush
EYES: small, brown, glass, black pupils
EARS: small, semi-circles, over face seams
MUZZLE: thin, cream, short, mohair plush

NOSE: hand-embroidered, rectangular, black
ARMS: small; cream, felt pads; black claws
FEET: small; oval, cream, felt pads; claws
STUFFING: wood-wool throughout bear

TRADEMARK: Originally, this bear would have come with a chest seal reading: "BE HA Quality Germany". This trademark was used from the firm's beginning until 1929.

⇒ "Gloria's Bear" ⇐

1920s SCHREYER & CO.

Originally owned by a child who sadly died in the 1920s, this tiny ted still lives with a small celluloid doll in the little girl's dolls' house, "Cliftonville" (now in a London museum). He is a particularly early example of the Schuco mascot bears, produced by the Nuremberg-based company, which was established in 1912.

Muzzle occupies most of the bear's face

Bear profile *From this angle, you can see the bear's extremely straight limbs and large head.*

EARS
His ears are made from tiny, half circles of card, covered with mohair plush. They are inserted into the seams along the top of the bear's head.

EYES
Black glass beads, probably on wire shanks, are used as eyes. These were common in small bears of the 1920s.

TRADEMARK
The Schuco trademark was formed from the first letters of the three words making up the company's German name: Schreyer und Co (Sch-u-co). Miniature bears were the company's speciality – in the 1920s, the average size of these bears was 6cm (2½ in).

Felt stuck to the end of the metal arm

PAWS
Made out of hand-shaped pieces of felt, the paws are a unique feature. Later Schuco bears had more conventional paws and feet, so these felt ones indicate a bear made between 1920 and 1940.

FEET
Small, V-shaped, metal slivers jut out from the ends of his legs, and are covered in beige felt to form the feet.

Beige felt paws

NOSE AND MOUTH
Horizontal stitches of black thread, shaped into a triangle, indicate his nose. The bear's mouth is also stitched.

Short and dense mohair plush is ideal for a small bear

LIMBS
The arms and legs are straight. They are jointed, using metal pins that pass through the top and bottom of the body. The flat-headed ends of the pins are just visible in the centre of the thigh and on the bear's upper arm.

STUFFING
"Gloria's Bear" is not stuffed in the usual way. A metal frame is covered with mohair plush, partly sewn and glued in place. This makes him feel extremely solid.

Felt has worn away on his feet, revealing the metal frame below

---

· BEAR ESSENTIALS ·

HT: 6cm (2½in)

FUR: golden, short-pile, mohair plush	NOSE: hand-embroidered, triangular, black	DISTINGUISHING FEATURES: The diminutive stature, metal frame, and unique felt paws, are the most distinctive features of this tiny bear.
EYES: small, black, glass beads	ARMS: straight; beige felt on paws; no claws	
EARS: tiny, half circles, along top of head	FEET: small; V-shaped, beige felt; no claws	
MUZZLE: blunt, protruding	STUFFING: internal metal frame	

❧ "Bertie" ❧

1930 DEAN'S RAG BOOK CO.

This bear was made by Britain's oldest existing soft toy manufacturers. Founded in 1903, and originally famous for their printed, cloth cut-out sheets of soft toys, Dean's began to make traditional, jointed, plush teddy bears in about 1915. "Bertie" was created at the height of their success.

EARS
His ears, made from two separate pieces of plush, are large and flat. They are placed quite a long way back from his face, so the inner edges align with the top of his flat head.

EYES
The translucent glass eyes are brown with black pupils. They have wire shanks which are sewn into place.

NOSE AND MOUTH
The nose is oval, and consists of vertical stitches. The wide and smiling mouth is represented by two single, horizontal stitches, sewn onto either side of a long, vertical chain stitch.

TRADEMARK
"Bertie" has a label, bearing the manufacturer's name, on his right paw. Some of Dean's early soft toys had metal buttons fixed to their bodies.

The remains of the worn label

Bear profile His large, triangular-shaped head, and relatively short, stumpy limbs represent the typical British bear shape.

The nose and mouth are embroidered in black thread

HEAD
"Bertie" has a large head with a wide forehead. His eyes are set half way down, while his muzzle gently tapers down from his face.

FEET
The short cotton pile of the velveteen pads has worn away, revealing the woven fabric and the beige, felt reinforcement underneath.

Fat, straight legs end in stubby feet

VOICE BOX
"Bertie" has a tilt growler which is still in working order.

• BEAR ESSENTIALS •

HT: 65cm (26in)

FUR: dark beige, soft, short, mohair plush
EYES: small, translucent, brown, glass
EARS: large, flat, set back and wide apart
MUZZLE: blunt, gently tapers from head

NOSE: hand-embroidered, oval, black
ARMS: stumpy; beige, velveteen pads; claws
FEET: stumpy; beige, velveteen pads; claws
STUFFING: wood-wool, wood-wool/kapok

MADE IN ENGLAND by Dean's Rag Book CO. LTD. LONDON

Trademark

⇜ Teddy Baby ⇝

1930 STEIFF

Originally designed in 1929, but rejected by the Patent Office, Steiff's successful Teddy Baby series was finally accepted the following year. He was advertised as a "life-like, comical, young bear-cub, whose friendly face speaks volumes", and he was produced in different sizes, materials, and colours. He remained popular up until the 1950s.

EARS
Teddy Baby has small, stiff ears, although his right one, here, has collapsed a little with time.

EYES
His brown glass eyes with black pupils have wire shanks, and are set in the seam which joins the clipped mohair muzzle to the main part of his head.

VOICE BOX
A large, oval squeaker, about 10cm (4in) long, can be felt inside Teddy Baby's long, fat tummy. Still working, it sounds more like a duck than a bear cub.

A printed swing tag and bell is attached to his collar

FUR
The main body of this Teddy Baby is covered in an attractive, peach cotton plush. (His muzzle is clipped mohair plush.) Other materials used for the production of this particular line included wool mohair and artificial silk plush in colours such as white, beige, dark brown, and an unusual blue.

Teddy Baby's large, flat feet resemble clowns' shoes

FEET
His feet are made of the same short, white, mohair plush as his muzzle. The woven, pink, cotton pads are reinforced with card.

Steiff button

Bear profile The unusually curved, S-shaped arms, particularly flat feet, protruding muzzle, and open mouth give him a distinctive profile.

Blue, leatherette collar, fastened at the back of the neck with a metal button

NOSE
The brown, vertical stitches are short on the outer edge, but become longer towards the centre, extending down to the top of the jaw.

MOUTH
The open mouth of this particular Teddy Baby reveals a flesh-coloured, felt palate. His chin is covered with a cream, clipped mohair plush, and the muzzle is of the same material but white. A few Teddy Babies were produced with closed mouths.

ACCESSORIES
Some bears were made with collars, a few had ribbon bows – and others wore nothing at all. Certain early versions were dressed in pink frocks and shoes, and lace-trimmed bibs.

• BEAR ESSENTIALS •

HT: 30cm (12in)

FUR: peach, cotton plush; clipped mohair
EYES: medium, brown, glass, black pupils
EARS: small, curved, stiff and set upright
MUZZLE: protruding, open mouth, clipped

NOSE: hand-embroidered, heart, brown
ARMS: tapering; pink, cotton pads; claws
FEET: large, flat; pink, cotton pads; claws
STUFFING: wood-wool throughout bear

Trademark

RUPERT BEAR

In November 1920, the Daily Express, a national newspaper, introduced Rupert Bear to British children. By the time the "Rupert League" was formed in 1932, Rupert had become a national institution. The League's aims were "… to be cheerful, unselfish and to strive … to make people happy." His appeal was universal, and through the famous Rupert Bear annuals, he became known in some twenty different countries. Soon Rupert Bear memorabilia was produced, and he was used often as a mascot for fundraising campaigns.

△ **Mary Tourtel**
The creator of Rupert.

RUPERT'S ADVENTURES

Rupert Bear was the creation of Mary Tourtel, a children's book illustrator. Mary's husband, an editor on the *Daily Express*, had been looking for a comic strip to rival those of other national newspapers. Rupert Bear ended the search. Mary Tourtel set her stories in an idyllic, timeless town, called Nutwood where Rupert became regularly involved in fairytale adventures featuring witches, ogres, and dragons. He also had a set of loveable and imaginatively named friends: Bill Badger, Algy Pug, Edward Trunk, and the Wise Old Goat.

A CONTINUING TRADITION

In 1935, Mary Tourtel retired because of failing sight, but her work was continued by the magazine and book illustrator, Alfred Bestall. He drew the daily adventures in the newspaper for the next 30 years, and also, from 1936, the Rupert annuals. From 1965 to 1978, the cartoon film animator, Alex Cubie illustrated Rupert's adventures; Freddie Chaplain wrote the stories. Today Rupert is illustrated by John Harrold, and written by Ian Robinson.

▽ **Annuals**
Two Rupert Daily Express Annuals, dating from 1949 (left), and 1952 (right).

◁ **Marionette**
A Rupert marionette made in the late 1950s, by Pelham Puppets. Like the original drawings of Rupert, this bear has human hands.

▽ **Dutch Version**
Since the 1920s, Rupert had been popular in Holland. This set of four postcards, and envelope, illustrated by Mary Tourtel, are very rare. They are one of two series published in the mid 1920s. In Holland, Rupert was known as Bruintje Beer (Brown Bear) and his adventures appeared in the Dutch newspaper, Algameen Handelsblad.

▷ **Pop-up Bear**
Rupert Bear appeared in pop-up annuals published by the Daily Express. This 1931 annual shows Rupert in original clothes: a blue jumper, grey check trousers, and scarf.

BIRTH OF AN INDUSTRY

The first Rupert merchandise was the "Little Bear Embroidery Card" made in 1921. Two years later a play was produced based on Rupert's adventures. It was called *Rupert's Revenge* and was written for the Daily Express Women's Exhibition in London. From the 1960s, numerous soft toys (including a talking version by Pedigree Soft Toys, and a rubber Bendy Toy, by Newfeld Ltd.), puppets, board games, jigsaws, and money boxes, were made. Rupert's appearance in two cartoon series, shown on television in the 1970s and 1980s, and a video in 1984, accelerated his commerical appeal. In 1983, an organization, "The Followers of Rupert", was founded to maintain the purity of the Rupert tradition. Its 700 members thoughout the world receive the journal, *Nutwood*, twice a year. A collection of Rupert Bear artefacts are housed in the local museum of Mary Tourtel's home town, Canterbury, England.

▽ **1986 Rupert Bear**
A Real Soft Toys design.

△ **Rupert and the Frog Chorus**
A still from the 1984 cartoon made by animator Geoff Dunbar, and musician Paul McCartney.

◁ **Recording Artist**
A record produced by BBC television to celebrate the 50th anniversary of the Rupert Bear annuals.

❧ "Compton" ❧
1920s J.K. FARNELL

This bear's general shape and unusual claw markings suggest that he was probably manufactured by J.K. Farnell (Est. 1897), one of Britain's oldest soft toy companies. The absence of any trademarks, however, make positive identification of "Compton" difficult.

EARS

"Compton's" small ears sit wide apart at a slightly jaunty angle. The inner edges are sewn into his facial seams, while the outer edges align with the sides of his head.

EYES

The clear glass eyes, with painted backs, give "Compton" a wide-eyed, surprised look. They are on wire shanks, sewn into his face with strong thread.

CLAWS

The design for the bear's claws was used by W.J. Terry before 1920, and by Merrythought from 1930.

STUFFING

"Compton" is mainly stuffed with kapok, but he has some wood-wool in his muzzle and also around his joints.

Clipped muzzle

Bear profile *This angle, which displays the bear's protruding muzzle, humped back, and long limbs, emphasises the similarity between Farnell bears and Steiff bears.*

NOSE AND MOUTH

His nose is embroidered with vertical black thread stitches; the outer stitches are extra long, extending over the upper edge of the bear's slightly lop-sided nose. His mouth is an inverted V with stitching joining it to the nose.

ARMS

The long, tapering arms are like those seen on early Steiff bears. They curve upwards, at the point where the paws start.

Joined claws are stitched across his felt pads

Long, narrow feet

Spoon-like pads of beige felt

• BEAR ESSENTIALS •

HT: 40cm (16in)

FUR: golden, slightly shaggy, mohair plush
EYES: medium, clear glass, painted backs
EARS: small, set wide apart
MUZZLE: blunt, protruding, clipped short

NOSE: hand-embroidered, black
ARMS: long, curved; beige, felt pads; claws
FEET: large, narrow; beige, felt pads; claws
STUFFING: wood-wool/kapok mixture

DISTINGUISHING FEATURES:
"Compton's" unusual joined claws, indicated with black thread and stitched across the beige felt pads, make him easily recognizable.

❧ "Chummy" ❧

1930-1935 MERRYTHOUGHT LTD.

"Chummy" is one of the earliest bears produced by Merrythought who, from 1930, began manufacturing soft toys near Ironbridge in Shropshire, England. Chad Valley's factory was not far away, and over the next ten years both companies produced similar cuddly, kapok-filled bears. Sometimes the bears are difficult to tell apart.

EARS
"Chummy" has large, flat, rounded ears similar to Chad Valley's "Mr Fluffy" (see p.43). Set quite far back, they are placed across the seams of his face.

EYES
The amber glass eyes with black pupils are on wire shanks, sewn into place through the seams of his face. They are set so low down that they accentuate "Chummy's" large forehead.

Golden, mohair plush

STUFFING
Like most British bears of this period, "Chummy" is stuffed with a kapok and wood-wool mix; his limbs are all kapok.

FEET
The feet are small and the ankles are thin when you compare them with the fat thighs. The foot pads on "Chummy" are felt, although Merrythought occasionally used brown velveteen on these bears.

Pointed, clipped muzzle

Bear profile *Notice "Chummy's" arms and the absence of a hump on his back – characteristics that distinguish the new-style British bear from early German bears.*

TRADEMARK
A celluloid button fixed into his left ear shows a wishbone; Merrythought is an old English word for wishbone.

VOICE BOX
"Chummy's" voice box no longer works.

CLAWS
The claws are typical of Merrythought bears of the period. Four are stitched across each felt pad, then their inner ends are joined with horizontal stitches.

A well-matched replacement felt pad

Joined claws

• BEAR ESSENTIALS •

HT: 57cm (23in)

FUR: golden, slightly shaggy, mohair plush
EYES: large, amber, glass, black pupils
EARS: large, flat, high on back of head
MUZZLE: pointed, facing down, clipped

NOSE: hand-embroidered, rectangular
ARMS: long, curved; rust, felt pads; claws
FEET: medium, oval, rust, felt pads; claws
STUFFING: kapok, wood-wool/kapok

Trademark

❧ "Colin" ❧

1930-1935 MERRYTHOUGHT LTD.

"Colin" is part of the Magnet Line, the first series of teddy bears produced by Merrythought in the early 1930s. Like the previous Merrythought bear (see p.53), he has a celluloid button, although this is fixed to his back and not to his left ear. The firm was forced to revise the button's position, as it copied Steiff's "button in ear".

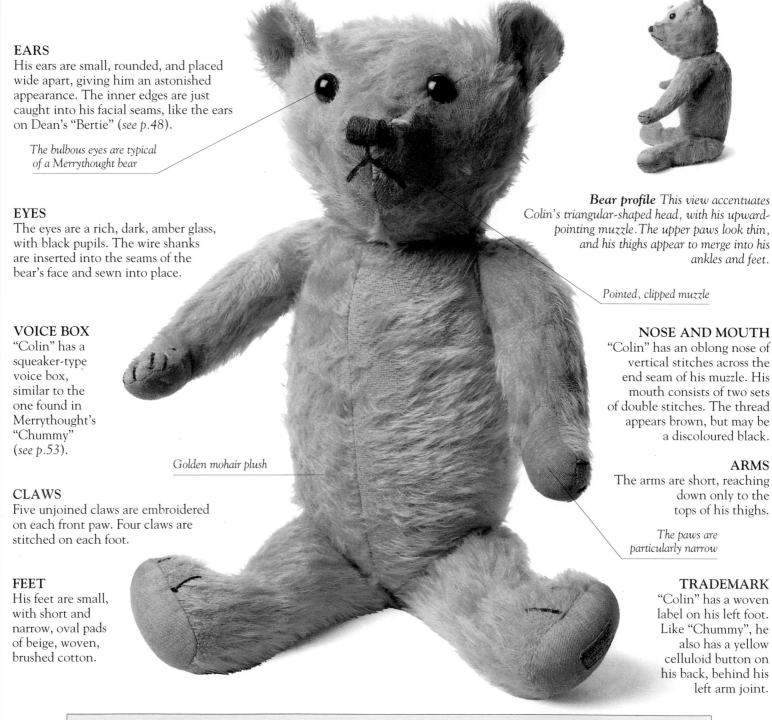

EARS
His ears are small, rounded, and placed wide apart, giving him an astonished appearance. The inner edges are just caught into his facial seams, like the ears on Dean's "Bertie" (*see p.48*).

The bulbous eyes are typical of a Merrythought bear

EYES
The eyes are a rich, dark, amber glass, with black pupils. The wire shanks are inserted into the seams of the bear's face and sewn into place.

VOICE BOX
"Colin" has a squeaker-type voice box, similar to the one found in Merrythought's "Chummy" (*see p.53*).

Golden mohair plush

CLAWS
Five unjoined claws are embroidered on each front paw. Four claws are stitched on each foot.

FEET
His feet are small, with short and narrow, oval pads of beige, woven, brushed cotton.

Bear profile *This view accentuates Colin's triangular-shaped head, with his upward-pointing muzzle. The upper paws look thin, and his thighs appear to merge into his ankles and feet.*

Pointed, clipped muzzle

NOSE AND MOUTH
"Colin" has an oblong nose of vertical stitches across the end seam of his muzzle. His mouth consists of two sets of double stitches. The thread appears brown, but may be a discoloured black.

ARMS
The arms are short, reaching down only to the tops of his thighs.

The paws are particularly narrow

TRADEMARK
"Colin" has a woven label on his left foot. Like "Chummy", he also has a yellow celluloid button on his back, behind his left arm joint.

• BEAR ESSENTIALS •

HT: 50cm (20in)

FUR: golden, threadbare mohair plush
EYES: bulbous, dark amber, glass, black pupils
EARS: small, erect, set wide apart in face seams
MUZZLE: pointed, turning upwards, clipped

NOSE: hand-embroidered, oblong, brown
ARMS: short; beige, cotton pads; claws
FEET: small; beige, cotton pads; claws
STUFFING: wood-wool and kapok mixture

Trademark

❧ Bingie ❧

1930s MERRYTHOUGHT LTD.

Bingie was part of a family of novelty teddies, produced by Merrythought throughout the 1930s. He represents a sitting bear cub who, with his extremely soft filling and short, unjointed legs, was intended to appeal to very young children. He was manufactured in seven sizes, with two extra-small sizes for babies, known as "Baby Bingie".

EARS
The back of each ear is made from the same mohair plush as the body, while the inner part is white, now discoloured, artifical silk plush.

EYES
Bingie has large, amber, glass eyes, positioned either side of the central seam, low down on his face.

Short, stocky, swivel-jointed arms

STUFFING
He is particularly cuddly as he is stuffed with kapok. Fine wood-wool is used as reinforcement behind the pads.

LEGS
His short, stocky legs are unjointed. They are sewn onto his body at an angle of 90°, so he is permanently in the sitting posture.

Pads wider at heels and toes

Bear profile The large head, rounded back, and huge feet, are all characteristics modelled on a real-life bear cub.

Clipped mohair muzzle

NOSE AND MOUTH
Vertical stitches of brown thread make up the large rectangular nose. Some long stitches reach from the tip of his muzzle down to his wide, stitched mouth.

Claws extend across plush and felt pads

CLAWS
Double stitching, in brown thread matching the nose and mouth, respresent claws on the feet and paws.

Shaggy cream mohair, tipped brown

• BEAR ESSENTIALS •

FUR: brown-tipped cream, shaggy, mohair
EYES: large, amber, glass, black pupils
EARS: large, flat, placed high on head
MUZZLE: long, separate piece, clipped

NOSE: hand-embroidered, rectangular, brown
ARMS: short, stocky; rust, felt pads; claws
FEET: large, long; rust, felt pads; claws
STUFFING: kapok; fine wood-wool in feet

HT: 35cm (14in)

Trademark

WINNIE THE POOH

Winnie the Pooh is probably the most well-known fictional bear in the world. Millions of copies of the book bearing his name as the title have been sold since it was first published by Methuen on 14th October 1926. It was subsequently translated into 22 languages, including Latin and Esperanto. Walt Disney made three very successful cartoon films featuring the bear and his friends. Winnie the Pooh stories have even been used to explain the principles of Taoism and, rather surprisingly, there is a street in Poland named after him.

Pooh

THE EARLY YEARS

Winnie the Pooh started life as a real teddy bear, bought from the famous London store, Harrods, in 1921, by Dorothy Milne, wife of the author, Alan Alexander Milne, for their son Christopher Robin's first birthday. The bear probably came from the factory of J.K. Farnell, as they made bears exclusively for Harrods at the time. Winnie the Pooh's original name was "Edward Bear". He first appeared in 1924, in A.A. Milne's anthology of poetry for children, *When We Were Very Young*. His name was later changed to Winnie the Pooh. The name "Winnie" came from an American black bear in London Zoo, the mascot of a Canadian regiment from Winnipeg; "Pooh" was the name of Christopher Robin's favourite swan. In 1925, the Milne's moved from their London home to Cotchford Farm in Sussex, close to Ashdown Forest. The area became the setting of many of the stories, and is visited today by devotees.

◁ *Happy Family*
A.A. Milne, his six year-old son Christopher Robin, and Winnie the Pooh, photographed in 1926.

△ *A Bear and his Honey*
This 1926 Shepard illustration shows Pooh protecting his honey from a flood.

△ *Final Home*
The original Winnie the Pooh is now in the New York Public Library.

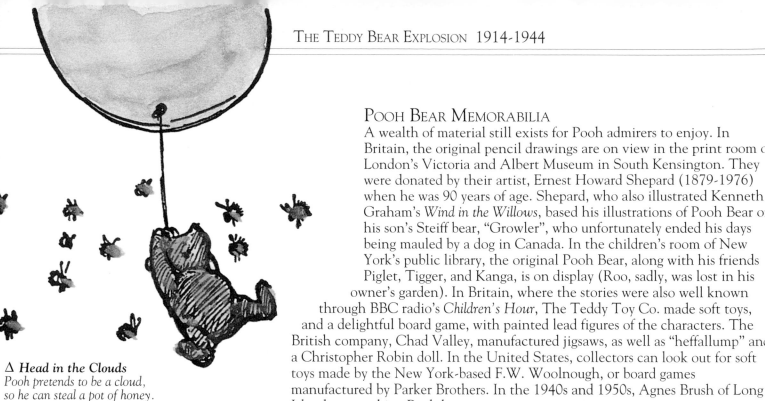

△ Head in the Clouds
Pooh pretends to be a cloud,
so he can steal a pot of honey.

POOH BEAR MEMORABILIA

A wealth of material still exists for Pooh admirers to enjoy. In Britain, the original pencil drawings are on view in the print room of London's Victoria and Albert Museum in South Kensington. They were donated by their artist, Ernest Howard Shepard (1879-1976) when he was 90 years of age. Shepard, who also illustrated Kenneth Graham's *Wind in the Willows*, based his illustrations of Pooh Bear on his son's Steiff bear, "Growler", who unfortunately ended his days being mauled by a dog in Canada. In the children's room of New York's public library, the original Pooh Bear, along with his friends Piglet, Tigger, and Kanga, is on display (Roo, sadly, was lost in his owner's garden). In Britain, where the stories were also well known through BBC radio's *Children's Hour*, The Teddy Toy Co. made soft toys, and a delightful board game, with painted lead figures of the characters. The British company, Chad Valley, manufactured jigsaws, as well as "heffallump" and a Christopher Robin doll. In the United States, collectors can look out for soft toys made by the New York-based F.W. Woolnough, or board games manufactured by Parker Brothers. In the 1940s and 1950s, Agnes Brush of Long Island, was making Pooh bears.

WALT DISNEY'S POOH BEAR

Winnie the Pooh's popularity was renewed with the launching of a twenty minute musical cartoon, *Winnie the Pooh and the Honey Tree*, by the Walt Disney studios in 1966. This was soon followed by *Winnie the Pooh and the Blustery Day*, and *Winnie the Pooh and Tigger Too*. In 1975, the three cartoons were combined to make a full-length feature film which proved then, as it is still today, immensely popular. Walt Disney's films meant that children growing up in this period knew a different kind of Pooh from their parents and grandparents. This was a Pooh Bear that talked with an American accent, provided by the actor Sterling Holloway. He was plumper than the original Pooh and he wore a red jacket. Disney bought the rights to the character and licensed various companies to reproduce Winnie the Pooh as a soft toy. In 1988, the first annual Walt Disney World Teddy Bear Convention was held in Florida, the United States.

▽ New Lease of Life for Drawings
Pooh is rescued by Christopher Robin and friends
from Rabbit's burrow, after eating too much honey
and condensed milk. Although he was well into his
nineties in 1973-1974, Methuen commissioned the
artist, E.H. Shepard, to give a new colour wash to
his original illustrations.

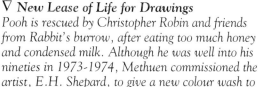

△ His Real Home
Pooh's house was in fact a hollow
walnut tree in A.A. Milne's garden.
This was a favourite place for
Christopher Robin and his bear.

❧ "Alex" ❧

c.1930 CHAD VALLEY

"Alex" has a button in his right ear. The Chad Valley button, which is celluloid over a metal base, is like the one used by Merrythought, one of Chad Valley's chief British rivals. One of the first directors of Merrythought originally worked for Chad Valley – so perhaps he took the idea to Merrythought.

EARS
Like "Mr Fluffy" *(see p.43)*, "Alex" has large, flat ears. They are set quite close together along the top and upper sides of his head.

Protruding, but blunt muzzle covered with clipped mohair

EYES
Amber, glass eyes on wire shanks make this bear typical of his period. A touch of glue has also been added for extra strength, a common practice at this time.

ARMS
His long, curved, and tapering arms end in large pads of brown brushed cotton.

Large feet with pads of brown, brushed cotton, reinforced with card

Bear profile *Although reminiscent of the more traditional German bear, "Alex" is much plumper, a common feature of British bears belonging to this period.*

The black thread used for the nose has faded to brown

NOSE
Vertical stitches, with a horizontal stitch across the top, make up the nose.

STUFFING
The limbs are all kapok; the body and head are filled with a mixture of kapok and wood-wool.

Long, mohair plush fur

• BEAR ESSENTIALS •

HT: 42cm (17in)

FUR: golden, long, curly, mohair plush
EYES: medium, amber, glass, black pupils
EARS: large, flat, close together, top of head
MUZZLE: blunt, protruding, clipped mohair

NOSE: hand-embroidered, triangular, black
ARMS: long; brown, brushed cotton pads; claws
FEET: large; brown, brushed cotton pads; claws
STUFFING: kapok and wood-wool mix/kapok

Printed lettering

Trademark

"Heinrich"

c.1935 SCHREYER & CO.

"Heinrich" is an example of a Schuco Yes/No bear. He has a moving head, operated by his tail which acts as a lever. Adolf Kahn, the Jewish partner of the Schuco firm, escaped to England from Germany in 1934, and may well have passed the idea on to H.G. Stone for their Chiltern Wagmee series of 1937.

Large, rounded ears centred across the facial seams

EYES
The main rims of his staring eyes are clear glass, painted mustard-yellow on the backs. They are inset with maroon pupils that have a white glass surround.

VOICE BOX
The squeaker mechanism inside his long, rounded, wood-wool stuffed body no longer works.

TRADEMARK
Schuco Yes/No bears usually have a printed Schuco card on their chests, but "Heinrich" has lost his.

TAIL
His tail consists of a loop of thick wire which extends from a hole in his lower back. The wire continues up inside the bear's body, where it is connected to the head's ball and socket joint. Using his tail, you can make his head move from side to side, or up and down.

Feet become wider at the toes

FEET
The dusty pink velveteen pads have been reinforced with stiff card. The toes and heels are a darker shade of pink.

Bear profile "Heinrich's" unusual tail *and downward curving arms, his short, stumpy legs, large feet, and open mouth, give him a distinctive profile.*

Wide, oval nose suggested with vertical, black thread stitches

MOUTH
The open mouth adds to the bear's slightly manic expression. Both his jaws are lined with pink felt; a separate piece of the same felt is glued to the back of his mouth to represent the tongue.

ARMS
His long, wide arms curve down at the paw ends (on traditional bears they curve upwards). Like his head and body, his arms are stuffed with wood-wool.

The feet and paws each have four claws stitched in black thread on the mohair plush

---

• BEAR ESSENTIALS •

FUR: honey-coloured, mohair plush
EYES: clear glass, yellow backs, maroon pupils
EARS: large, rounded, centred in face seams
HT: 34cm (13½in) MUZZLE: blunt, protruding; open mouth

NOSE: hand-embroidered, wide, oval, black
ARMS: large; pink, velveteen pads; claws
FEET: wide; pink, velveteen pads; claws
STUFFING: wood-wool throughout bear

Trademark

❧ "Miss Jessie Criddle" ❧

1930s F.W. WOOLWORTH

"Miss Jessie Criddle" was originally bought in a Woolworth store in England before World War II. F.W. Woolworth was an American chain that opened its first store in Britain in 1909; by the early 1930s there were branches in most major towns. Made from low-quality plush, she is typical of the cheaper range of British bears at the time.

EARS
"Miss Jessie Criddle's" flat ears are large and floppy, because they are made from thin plush. They sit towards the back of her head.

HEAD
The large, domed head has a rounded, jutting-out chin, that makes her muzzle quite unique.

Patch under right armpit

EYES
Her amber glass eyes are on wire hooks. Placed wide apart, they are sewn into the facial seam. Similar bears dating from the 1950s, had plastic eyes on wire shanks.

STUFFING
The rather dark shade of wood-wool, seen poking though holes in the paw pads, indicates that "Miss Jessie Criddle" is a low-quality bear.

FUR
"Miss Jessie Criddle" shows signs of wear and tear, and love and affection: her artificial silk plush fur is well-worn for her age.

Thin curved paws

FEET
This bear's feet are large, rounded and stocky. They are similar in shape to "Colin's" (*see p.54*).

Bear profile At this angle, you can see the bear's unusual, protruding chin, and rather short arms and feet. "Miss Jessie Criddle's" narrow hips are typical of a 1930s British bear.

NOSE
Her nose is embroidered with black wool, vertical stitches. Two of the centre stitches extend down to her mouth.

ARMS
The short, tapering arms are particularly wide near the shoulder. Her paws are covered in dark brown Rexine (oilcloth).

Short, artificial silk plush

CLAWS
Note that neither her feet nor her paws have embroidered claws, a feature that distinguishes her from earlier bears.

Well worn Rexine pads

• BEAR ESSENTIALS •

HT: 73cm (29in)

FUR: golden, short, artificial silk plush
EYES: medium, amber, glass, black pupils
EARS: large, flat, floppy, towards back of head
MUZZLE: square, protruding, jutting chin

NOSE: hand-embroidered, square, black
ARMS: short; brown, Rexine pads; no claws
FEET: stocky; brown, Rexine pads; no claws
STUFFING: wood-wool throughout bear

DISTINGUISHING FEATURES: "Miss Jessie Criddle" has particularly large and floppy ears, owing to the thinness of the plush. The ears sit at the back of the head.

❧ "Mr Jollyboy" ❧

LATE 1930s BRITISH

"Mr Jollyboy" is very similar to "Miss Jessie Criddle" (see p.60), and may have been made in the same factory. He is a fine example of the numerous bears of coloured, artificial silk plush that were produced in contrast to the more common shades of brown. These coloured bears were made well into the 1950s, and are sometimes difficult to date.

EARS
His small, flat ears sit firmly in the corners of his rather large, square head.

EYES
"Mr Jollyboy" has brown, glass eyes on straight, wire shanks, inserted into the facial seams. They are set wide apart and low down, giving the bear a broad and deep forehead.

FUR
The artificial silk (rayon plush), was woven out of fibres made from reconstituted cellulose, derived from wood. This early, man-made fabric was probably introduced to the soft toy industry by the British United Toy Manufacturing Co..

VOICE BOX
Like "Miss Jessie Criddle", "Mr Jollyboy" has a tilt growler deep inside his cavernous chest.

Short, stocky feet with Rexine pads

Long, narrow, stitched nose

Bear profile *Viewed from the side, his large, rounded head and body, short, stocky limbs, and slightly jutting-out chin are particularly noticeable.*

NOSE AND MOUTH
The nose consists of a few vertical stitches of black, woollen thread in contrast to the wide, square-shaped nose so often seen on other bears. The mouth is a gently curving line.

ARMS
The arms are short, stumpy, and of much the same thickness all the way along. They curve slightly at the paw ends, which are defined by beige-coloured, Rexine pads.

The absence of claws sometimes suggests a low-quality bear

• BEAR ESSENTIALS •

HT: 70cm (28in)

FUR: pale blue, woven artificial silk plush
EYES: small, brown, glass, placed wide apart
EARS: small, flat, in corners of square head
MUZZLE: square, large, with protruding chin

NOSE: hand-embroidered, long, thin, black
ARMS: short; beige, Rexine pads; no claws
FEET: short; beige, Rexine pads; no claws
STUFFING: wood-wool throughout bear

DISTINGUISHING FEATURES: The artificial silk plush along with the unusual, vertical nose, and jutting-out chin, differentiate this bear from his contemporaries.

❧ "Arthur van Gelden" ❧

1930s DUTCH

"Arthur van Gelden's" present owner bought him from a Dutch dealer. As he is similar to other bears of Dutch origin, it is assumed that he was made in Holland. In appearance, he could be confused with cheap range English bears of the same period, but his immense weight distinguishes him from them.

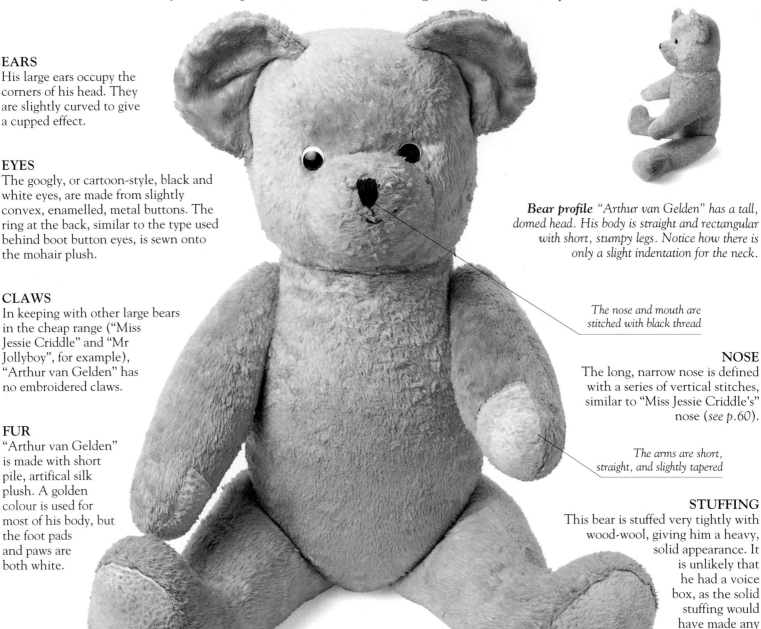

EARS
His large ears occupy the corners of his head. They are slightly curved to give a cupped effect.

EYES
The googly, or cartoon-style, black and white eyes, are made from slightly convex, enamelled, metal buttons. The ring at the back, similar to the type used behind boot button eyes, is sewn onto the mohair plush.

CLAWS
In keeping with other large bears in the cheap range ("Miss Jessie Criddle" and "Mr Jollyboy", for example), "Arthur van Gelden" has no embroidered claws.

FUR
"Arthur van Gelden" is made with short pile, artifical silk plush. A golden colour is used for most of his body, but the foot pads and paws are both white.

Large, rounded feet

Bear profile "Arthur van Gelden" has a tall, domed head. His body is straight and rectangular with short, stumpy legs. Notice how there is only a slight indentation for the neck.

The nose and mouth are stitched with black thread

NOSE
The long, narrow nose is defined with a series of vertical stitches, similar to "Miss Jessie Criddle's" nose (*see p.60*).

The arms are short, straight, and slightly tapered

STUFFING
This bear is stuffed very tightly with wood-wool, giving him a heavy, solid appearance. It is unlikely that he had a voice box, as the solid stuffing would have made any noise inaudible.

• BEAR ESSENTIALS •

HT: 70cm (28in)

FUR: golden, short, artificial silk plush
EYES: medium, enamelled, metal buttons
EARS: large, rounded, slightly cupped
MUZZLE: blunt, protruding, upward curve

NOSE: hand-embroidered, narrow, black
ARMS: straight; white, plush pads; no claws
FEET: large, rounded; white pads; no claws
STUFFING: very compact wood-wool

DISTINGUISHING FEATURES: "Arthur van Gelden" is a solid, heavy, teddy bear. His enamelled button eyes, narrow nose, and white pads all help with identification.

❧ "Marcel" ❧

1920s FRENCH

The majority of teddy bears for sale in France were imported from Germany, until the limited supply caused by World War I stimulated the establishment of French factories. Rivalling Steiff, metal button trademarks were sometimes used in the ear or, as in the case of "Marcel", on the body, for identification.

EYES
The small, glass eyes have the remains of paint on their backs. They are held on wire shanks sewn into the bear's face.

Small, rounded ears are set across his facial seams towards the back of his head

VOICE BOX
An oval squeaker mechanism in "Marcel's" long, thin body still works.

FEET
His relatively large feet have thin ankles in the Steiff tradition. The brown felt used for the pads is a different shade to that used on the paws, although it is difficult to tell which of the two are replacements.

TRADEMARK
A gold metal button clipped to the bear's chest is an idea borrowed from Steiff. The French may also have copied the concept of a raised symbol from the German company. Illustrations of hugging bears appeared in Steiff catalogues dating from before World War I.

The ankles are very thin

Short, cinnamon-coloured mohair plush

Bear profile *From this angle you can see "Marcel's" long, thin body, large feet, narrow paws, and pointed muzzle, with an unusual squashed nose.*

NOSE AND MOUTH
The black stitching for the nose and mouth is at a slight angle and not very neat, indicating, perhaps, that it is the work of an untrained seamstress.

ARMS
The long, thin, tapering arms end in small, narrow paws with dark brown, felt pads.

CLAWS
There are three claws on each foot and each paw. They are stitched in black thread.

The claws are stitched across the mohair plush and brown felt

---

• BEAR ESSENTIALS •

HT: 38cm (15in)

FUR: cinnamon-coloured, short, mohair plush
EYES: small, glass, black-painted backs
EARS: small, curved, towards back of head
MUZZLE: thin, protruding, and pointed

NOSE: hand-embroidered, rectangular, black
ARMS: small; dark brown, felt pads; claws
FEET: large; brown, felt pads; claws
STUFFING: wood-wool throughout bear

Raised lettering and logo

Trademark

❧ "Didcock" ❧

1938 J.K. FARNELL

"Didcock", with his Alpha toy trademark, would have been manufactured at Farnell's west London factory. Built after World War I, the works were destroyed by fire in 1934, and rebuilt the following year, only to be razed to the ground in the Blitz of 1940. Despite two more moves, Alpha bears remained a popular line until 1968.

EARS
The ears are relatively large and slightly cupped.

Ears are partly concealed by the shaggy fur

EYES
"Didcock" has unusual black button eyes. Said by his owner to be original, they add greatly to his charm and appeal.

ARMS
He has long, tapering arms, based on the traditional teddy bear style. They are distinctly curved at the paw ends, making them lie gracefully in his lap.

STUFFING
His head and arms are stuffed with wood-wool, and his legs are filled with kapok. His body is filled with a mixture of both materials.

The feet are large compared with the short legs

Bear profile *The side view demonstrates that Farnell followed the traditional teddy bear shape based on Steiff, rather than the one introduced by their rivals in Britain.*

NOSE
His square nose consists of vertical stitches of black thread. His crooked mouth makes him look bemused.

Claws are embroidered on each paw and foot with black thread

TRADEMARK
The woven label has the Alpha trademark, registered in 1925.

❖ BEAR ESSENTIALS ❖

HT: 38cm (15in)

FUR: long, blond, curly mohair plush
EYES: small, black, plastic buttons
EARS: large, slightly cupped and concealed
MUZZLE: protruding from flat forehead

NOSE: hand-embroidered, square, black
ARMS: curved; beige, cotton pads; claws
FEET: large; beige, cotton pads; claws
STUFFING: wood-wool, kapok and mix

Trademark

❧ "Senior Mr Roosevelt" ❧

c.1940 KNICKERBOCKER TOY CO. INC.

This American company had been making soft toys and bears since the early 1900s. Originally based in New York (where this bear was made), the firm later moved to New Jersey, and imported their sewn component parts from Korea. Although the firm no longer exists, they are noted for their Smokey bears, made in the 1960s and 1970s.

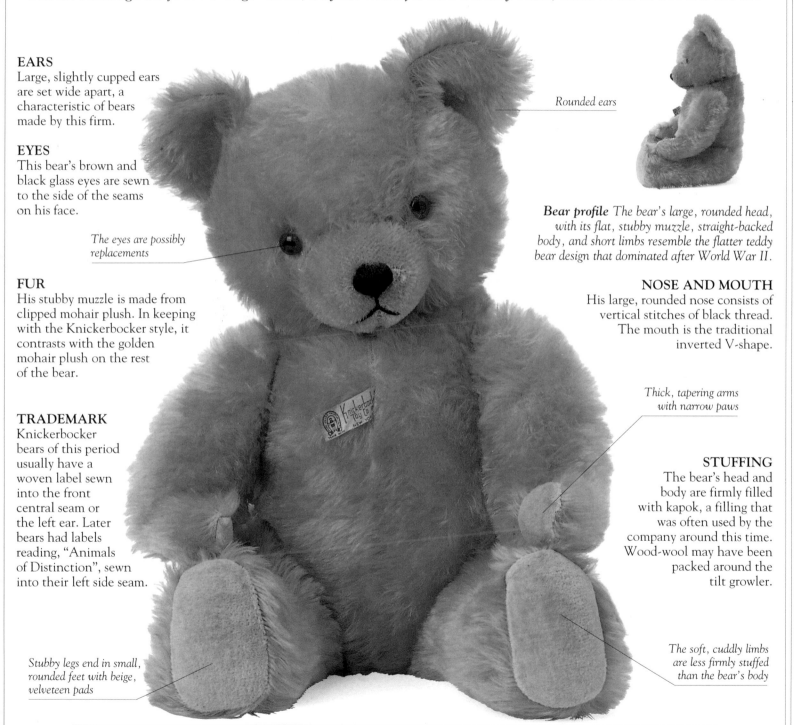

EARS
Large, slightly cupped ears are set wide apart, a characteristic of bears made by this firm.

EYES
This bear's brown and black glass eyes are sewn to the side of the seams on his face.

The eyes are possibly replacements

FUR
His stubby muzzle is made from clipped mohair plush. In keeping with the Knickerbocker style, it contrasts with the golden mohair plush on the rest of the bear.

TRADEMARK
Knickerbocker bears of this period usually have a woven label sewn into the front central seam or the left ear. Later bears had labels reading, "Animals of Distinction", sewn into their left side seam.

Stubby legs end in small, rounded feet with beige, velveteen pads

Rounded ears

Bear profile The bear's large, rounded head, with its flat, stubby muzzle, straight-backed body, and short limbs resemble the flatter teddy bear design that dominated after World War II.

NOSE AND MOUTH
His large, rounded nose consists of vertical stitches of black thread. The mouth is the traditional inverted V-shape.

Thick, tapering arms with narrow paws

STUFFING
The bear's head and body are firmly filled with kapok, a filling that was often used by the company around this time. Wood-wool may have been packed around the tilt growler.

The soft, cuddly limbs are less firmly stuffed than the bear's body

---

• BEAR ESSENTIALS •

HT: 51cm (20in)

FUR: golden mohair plush, clipped mohair
EYES: small, brown and black, glass, wide-set
EARS: large, rounded, cupped, set wide apart
MUZZLE: short, rounded, blunt, clipped

NOSE: hand-embroidered, oval, black
ARMS: short; beige, velveteen pads; no claws
FEET: small; beige, velveteen pads; no claws
STUFFING: kapok and wood-wool

Trademark

❧ "Edward" ❧

1940s AUSTRALIAN OR BRITISH

Now living in a vicarage in the south of England, "Edward" was his owner's friend and companion during her childhood in Australia. He is made of sheepskin, dyed golden brown, and he is a typical example of a teddy bear produced during World War II, when traditional mohair plush was in short supply.

EARS
These are made of two narrow, semi-circles of sheepskin, sewn into the corners of his square-shaped head.

Golden-brown sheepskin

EYES
His eyes are made of clear glass. Tiny amounts of paint suggest they were once painted brown on the backs. The pupils are black. The wire shanks are sewn onto his face with thick thread, which is knotted at the back of his head.

VOICE BOX
This bear's tilt growler is made of an early, mottled, green plastic. The base is marked, "Kim Toys Made in England", although it is possible that the voice box was imported to be used in an Australian-made bear. Alternatively, the whole toy may have been imported from England.

FEET
His feet show little ankle definition. The leather pads are oversewn with large stitches of black cotton – some may be repair work. He has no claws.

Short, oval, black leather pads

Unjointed head

Bear profile *Manufacturers tried to retain the traditional teddy bear design, but wartime shortages forced them to use thicker, less flexible materials. As a result of this, his back has no hump and his head is relatively flat.*

NOSE
The round, grey leather nose is probably a replacement for the original one that would have matched the bear's black leather pads. The new nose is larger than the original, perhaps covering worn sheepskin on the muzzle and mouth.

The tapered, curved arms are in the style of the contemporary British bears

JOINTS
"Edward" has small, cardboard disc joints in both his legs and arms. The bear has no head joint.

STUFFING
The head and limbs are filled with wood-wool. The body is a wood-wool and cotton waste wadding mix.

• BEAR ESSENTIALS •

HT: 53cm (21in)

FUR: golden-brown, dyed sheepskin
EYES: medium, clear glass, black pupils
EARS: narrow, semi-circles of sheepskin
MUZZLE: blunt, wide, slightly protruding

NOSE: grey leather replacement patch; large
ARMS: short; black, leather pads; no claws
FEET: small; black, leather pads; no claws
STUFFING: wood-wool, wood-wool/cotton

DISTINGUISHING FEATURES: Wartime shortages forced the manufacturers to use sheepskin for fur instead of the traditional woven mohair plush.

❧ "Chilli Pepper" ❧

1940s H.G. STONE & CO. LTD.

"Chilli" is an example of a Chiltern soft toy, so-called because the British firm's factory was in the Chiltern Hills of Buckinghamshire. He is a clockwork musical teddy bear belonging to their Hugmee range. He plays "Brahms' Lullaby" when wound up; earlier Chiltern teddies played tunes when their bodies were pressed.

EARS
His almost circular ears are positioned towards the back of his head. Set wide apart, the inner edges are turned slightly and caught in the seams of his face.

EYES
The amber glass eyes with black pupils are attached to short wire hooks. The hooks are sewn onto his face with strong white thread, which goes right through his head and is fastened at the back, near his neck.

VOICE BOX
The clockwork musical mechanism works on the Swiss comb and toothed-cylinder principle (*see p.37*). Housed in a square metal canister covered in white gauze, it is fitted into the lower back of his body. The key sticks out through a brass-like, metal eyelet on his back.

His colouring is an unusual coral pink

FUR
Unlike most bears in the Hugmee range, who were covered with mohair plush, "Chilli" is made with artificial silk plush. This man-made fabric was popular with certain other soft toy manufacturers at the time.

Bear profile This view shows the dents that mark where his eyes are fastened off at the back of his head, and the key to his internal music-box. Notice how his large, round muzzle occupies most of his face.

NOSE AND MOUTH
Hand-embroidered in black thread, his nose is rectangular. The small, inverted V of his mouth creates the characteristic glum expression of a Chiltern, Hugmee bear.

Relatively short arms

CLAWS
Four short claws of black thread are stitched to each paw. On the foot pads there are four claws, suggested with diagonal stitches reaching across the pad onto the artificial silk plush.

STUFFING
Cotton wadding makes "Chilli" cuddly and hygienic.

Beige velveteen pads on small feet

• BEAR ESSENTIALS •

HT: 42cm (16in)

FUR: coral pink, woven artificial silk plush
EYES: small, amber, glass with black pupils
EARS: rounded, wide apart, turned slightly
MUZZLE: large, rounded, short but wide

NOSE: hand-embroidered, rectangular, black
ARMS: short; beige, velveteen pads; claws
FEET: small; beige, velveteen pads; claws
STUFFING: pale blue cotton waste wadding

TRADEMARK: "Chilli Pepper" may once have had a small, fabric label, bearing the company's trade name, Chiltern Toys. It is possible that he also had a card swing tag.

SMOKEY THE BEAR

Smokey the Bear is the popular symbol that represents the Cooperative Forest Fire Prevention Campaign in the United States. He first appeared on a poster in 1944 with the message, "Smokey says: Care will prevent nine out of ten fires". He immediately won over the hearts of the American people. His popularity was boosted by the arrival at the zoo in Washington D.C., in 1950, of a bear cub that had been wounded in a fire, in New Mexico's Lincoln National Forest. He, too, was named Smokey.

△ *True Story*
Smokey the
Bear Book

CAMPAIGN AGAINST FOREST FIRES

In the 1940s, a spate of fires devastated large areas of forestation in the United States, making it essential to find a powerful new character to promote the Cooperative Forest Fire Prevention Campaign. A bear seemed the obvious choice; the forest was his natural habitat, and bears are known for their strength. The name "Smokey" was borrowed from Smokey Joe Martin, who worked for the New York City Fire Department during the 1920s. Albert Staehle, an artist with *The Saturday Evening Post*, was the original illustrator of Smokey, who became known as the "guardian of the forest". He portrayed the bear, putting out a campfire with a bucket of water, on a poster produced by the Wartime Advertising Council. The earliest illustrations of Smokey Bear show him undressed although it was not long before he was given his now familiar denim jeans and ranger hat. As the years went on, he became less bearlike.

▽ *Ideal Bear*
The first Smokey Bear was made by Ideal in 1953. He had a vinyl head, feet, and hands.

SMOKEY BEAR ACT

So great was his popularity, that in May 1952, the "Smokey Bear Act" was passed by Congress to protect the exploitation of the character. Only the United States Department of State Foresters and the Advertising Council could authorise the manufacture of Smokey products, with fees going towards the prevention of forest fires.

▷ *Smokey Artefacts*
A pair of child's binoculars – for spotting both wildlife and forest fires – has a leather case decorated with Smokey's face. Items like these are very popular with collectors today.

AN IMPORTANT BEAR
Some of the early licensed Smokey items, such as the Ideal Company's first Smokey soft toy (1953), and the second version with a vinyl face and all-in-one jeans, which followed a year later, are highly collectable. Ideal also invented an application form for proud Smokey owners to become a Junior Forest Rangers, a popular novelty, which resulted in the bear having his own address: Smokey Bear Headquarters, Washington DC., 20252. A third Ideal Smokey was introduced in the 1960s. Several other American firms, such as Dakin and the Knickerbocker Toy Co. produced their own versions during the 1960s and 1970s, including Smokey Bears that could talk and give advice about preventing forest fires.

SMOKEY COLLECTABLES
Moulded figurines, mugs, money boxes, ashtrays, clocks, clothing, and stationery are among the numerous Smokey Bear memorabilia that have been produced over the years. Educational posters were sold, including an early talking card poster, printed with the bear's face, which had a pull-string voice box on the reverse. Books and songs have been written about him and he continues to be a figure of great importance and popular appeal in the prevention of forest fires throughout the United States.

△ **1960s Version**
Ideal's third version of Smokey was created in the 1960s. It was made from plush with all-in-one jeans. Like earlier versions, he is instantly recognizable as he wears a Smokey Ranger badge, belt, and hat.

▽ **Ranger Hats**
A Smokey Bear ranger hat, available in child and adult sizes.

◁ **Take Care**
A Smokey Bear figurine, wearing denim jeans and carrying the familiar shovel. He has his hand raised in the "Take Care" pose.

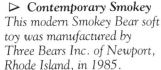

▷ **Contemporary Smokey**
This modern Smokey Bear soft toy was manufactured by Three Bears Inc. of Newport, Rhode Island, in 1985.

❧ THE SYNTHETIC TEDDY BEAR ❧

Although the years immediately after World War II saw a decrease in teddy bear production, the 1950s and 1960s witnessed the re-emergence of the teddy bear phenomenon. Bears made during this period were radically different from the pre-war designs. The ever increasing availability of new materials, as a result of pre-war developments in the field of plastics, revolutionized the industry. Various cartoon characters created by American animated film studios also stimulated some manufacturers to create bears that were caricatures, such as Merrythought's Cheeky (see p.83), as well as sophisticated gimmickry, like Dean's 1967 perfumed bear, Scenty Bear, and Chad Valley's 1968 pull-string, talking bear.

A NEW GENERATION

By 1960, many teddy bear manufacturers were using woven, and later knitted, nylon plush fabric. In Britain, for example, Dean's Childsplay, a subsidiary of Dean's Rag Book Co., offered a De-Luxe Bri-Nylon teddy bear in 1965. (Bri-Nylon was the registered trademark of ICI, which made several synthetic fabrics.) Another fabric, Acrilan, woven from an acrylic fibre, was produced by the American-owned Monsanto company. During this period, experiments were also underway to develop a safe plastic eye to replace the early eyes fixed so precariously to easily broken wire shanks. Wendy Boston Playsafe Toys patented a rust-proof screw locked eye in the late 1940s, which was later perfected using moulded nylon for both screw and nut.

THE MACHINE-WASHABLE BEAR

The use of artificial fabrics and plastic eyes made it possible for Wendy Boston to create the first completely machine-washable bear. Before this development, bears could not be immersed in water: sodden wood-wool was difficult to dry, damp kapok stained fabrics, and Rayon, too, did not take kindly to water. Nylon, in contrast, did, and combined with a water-repellent and quick-drying filling, such as polyurethane or latex foams in granular form, unbreakable eyes, and the omission of cardboard joints, the machine-washable bear was born. Wendy

△ Royal Bear
This was manufactured by Merrythought, in honour of Queen Elizabeth II's coronation in 1953.

▽ Machine-washable Bear
Wendy Boston nylon plush bears.

△ TV Appearance
The complete washability of the Wendy Boston bear was demonstrated on television in 1955.

◁ Fashion Bears
Mary Quant, 1960s trend-setter, with her own teddy bears.

Boston advertised the amazing breakthrough for the first time on television in 1955. This led to the phenomenon unique to a post-war generation – the teddy bear pegged to a washing line by his ears. The latter part of this teddy era saw the rise of American soft toy firms, such as Dakin, and Wallace Berrie, who contracted out much of their work to Far Eastern countries, such as Taiwan, Korea, and China, where labour was cheaper. Several famous names associated with the British teddy bear could not compete; by the late 1960s companies such as J.K. Farnell, Wendy Boston, and H.G. Stone had either folded or had been bought by larger companies. The increase in competition was also marked by the introduction of new equipment into soft toy factories so production could be stepped up. Wind-filling machines, for example, brought stuffing by hand to an end. In the new system, compressed air propelled the filling material through a narrow pipe, over which the opening of the teddy bear's limb, head, or body would be fitted. Some of these machines could fill toys 500 times faster than previously. Mechanical cutters that could stamp out several pieces of plush fabric at a time, replaced the old method of cutting out individual templates, and also helped improve factory efficiency.

△ Bri-Nylon
This tradename was registered in 1960.

▽ X-rayed Bear
An X-ray of an American tumbling bear, revealing that both plastic and metal have been used in the bear's internal structure.

△ The Ever-popular Teddy
After the war, the new-look teddy proved just as popular as the earlier designs.

NEW SAFETY STANDARDS

During this period, governments turned their attention to regulations regarding toy safety. The British Standards Institution, for example, issued several Codes of Safety between 1958 and 1968, offering recommendations and test requirements. As a result, teddy bears became the subject of arson attacks by white-coated scientists, experimenting with different yarns to produce inherently non-flammable fabrics or searching for flame-resistant solutions for their treatment. Heavy weights of 30 lbs (15 kg), or more, were secured to teddy bears' eyes to see whether they would withstand removal by human finger nails or teeth. Hygiene was also an issue, and new regulations demanded the testing of stuffings to determine cleanliness. As a result, many teddy bears boasted possession of a "Certificate of Hygiene".

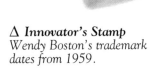

△ Innovator's Stamp
Wendy Boston's trademark dates from 1959.

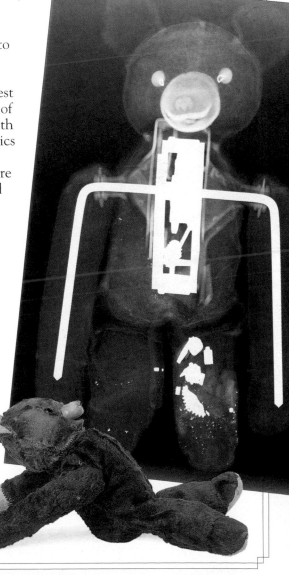

▽ Tumbling Bear
Wind up this bear's arm and see him tumble.

BEAR NECESSITIES

Rationing continued to create shortages immediately after World War II, but soon teddy bear manufacturing was revolutionized by the use of synthetic materials. With the help of new technology, as well as a greater awareness of safety standards, soft toy producers began to create the first completely man-made, fully washable, almost indestructible teddy bear.

Leg joint disc

Arm joint disc

Hardboard discs with plastic pin

Hardboard discs with cotter pin

Cardboard disc with metal washer

JOINTS
Jointing systems continued to be made with cardboard or hardboard discs and metal washers, although manufacturers experimented with the use of plastic for both the discs and pins.

1960s synthetic plush

Golden mohair plush

1950s acrylic plush

c.1965 BRITISH
A bear made by Pedigree Soft Toys Ltd., with woven, Bri-nylon plush, plastic foam stuffing, and safe lock-in plastic eyes.

Glass eye

Plastic eyes

Wendy Boston eye

Plastic safe eye

NOSE
Black, moulded rubber noses were first introduced on some bears in the 1950s.

PLASTIC EYES
By the 1950s, plastic eyes were common. Wendy Boston patented their screw-in, moulded, nylon eye in 1948. Similar plastic eyes followed. The safe lock-in eyes had washers; some of the earlier plastic eyes had wire shanks; later ones had plastic shanks with washers.

FUR
After World War II, many manufacturers turned to synthetic fabrics, such as acrylic and nylon plush, which could be made in various colours and piles. Natural, mohair plush was still used, however.

Hollow globe of metal alloy holds small, lead-like pellet

BELL
In 1957, Merrythought made a bear with a bell in each ear; other firms copied them throughout the late 1950s and early 1960s.

THREAD
Synthetic-based threads, such as nylon and polyester, began to replace cottons for machine-stitching.

Synthetic-based thread

Cotton thread

Sheepskin

Wood-wool

DETAILS
Noses, mouths and claws were mostly embroidered in the traditional way, with black or brown thread.

Synthetic plush

Suedette

PAD FABRICS
Traditional style bears continued to have pads made from felt, and Rexine faded out in the late 1950s. Woven cotton fabric and velveteen remained popular until the 1960s, when it was replaced by synthetic equivalents, such as suedette. Manufacturers of unjointed, washable teddy bears used the same synthetic plush for the pads as the rest of the body, but chose a differing colour or pile (in the past a contrasting fabric was used).

Rexine

Woven cotton fabric

Velveteen

Felt

Cardboard

REINFORCED PADS
Many bears produced in the traditional style continued to have foot and paw pads reinforced with cardboard.

Embroidery thread

GROWLERS
Tilt growlers with sliding, weighted bellows remained popular during this period; the cardboard canisters often had perforated tin "speakers". Cardboard lids were still used, and all-plastic containers became available from the 1940s. Cardboard and oilcloth squeakers remained almost unchanged, but for the occasional use of the external reed encased in cardboard.

Tin speaker

Squeaker with external reed

Squeakers with internal reeds

STUFFING
Wood-wool and kapok, and kapok substitute (sub) made from the waste of textile mills, were still used. By the 1950s, however, many manufacturers were turning to plastic foam, a wholly synthetic, sponge-like substance (usually shredded), that helped them to create the machine washable teddy bear.

Kapok

Shredded plastic foam

Sub

MUSICAL BOX
The traditional Swiss clockwork movement was still commonly used, although a moulded, nylon cover often replaced the all-metal casing.

Musical box with plastic cover

BEAR APPAREL

In the years following World War II, teddy's wardrobe was less imaginative as manufacturers were restricted in the types of materials they could use. During this period, the teddy bear's shape changed. His head became enormous and his limbs short and stumpy, making him difficult to clothe stylishly. Less and less clothes were made professionally, and the teddy bear tended to depend on dolls' cast-offs, or a young owner's first tentative knitting skills. Many teddy bears were made with soft, colourful, synthetic fabrics, and this, combined with an increasingly un-bearlike shape, led to their role as a tactile comforter, rather than as a character with a costume. Today's collectors often make their teddys' clothes themselves.

ALL-IN-ONE BEAR

Many of the dressed bears prevalent in the years before World War II were still being made during the 1950s, which can sometimes make dating difficult for collectors. Teddy bears with all-in-one clothes and bodies were particularly common during this period of economic stringency. It enabled manufacturers to save on plush, although it meant that children would, and indeed did, miss out on the dressing and the undressing of their teddy bears. Although the teddy bear lacked exquisite dress sense in this period, many companies made some effort to dress their teddy bears in some style. The Paris company, ALFA, had been making all-in-one teddy bears since 1935, and in the 1950s they were offering particularly feminine bears. These bears would be dressed in blue or red gingham dresses, trimmed with lace and ribbon, and wearing matching slippers.

△ **Tartan Ted**
A sheepskin bear in tartan.

THE CHEEKY DYNASTY

Across the Channel, in England, Merrythought's Cheeky bear, first introduced in 1957 (*see p.83*), was produced with a woven fabric body and limbs that represented clothes. However the trousers and braces, and pinafore and dress, worn by Mr and Mrs Twisty Cheeky of 1966-68, with their unique internal wire frames that could bend in all directions, could be removed from their suede bodies.

◁ **Indian Attire**
"Kensington" dates from 1918, although he wears a stunning embroidered and bespangled child's jacket, which was bought in the north Indian state of Uttar, Pradesh, in the 1960s.

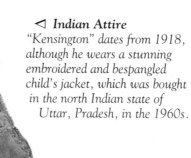

△ **Rupert Bear Look-alike**
With his knitted red sweater, and yellow-checked trousers, he is dressed to resemble the cartoon character, Rupert Bear.

A STEP BACK

Steiff reintroduced some teddy bears in the 1950s that had originally been produced before World War II. Teddyli, who had a head of either dark brown or blond plush and an open or closed mouth, was based directly on Teddy Baby of the 1930s (see p.49). Teddyli's soft fabric body with dangling, unstuffed arms and straight, standing feet, however, make him unique to this period. He came dressed in a variety of delightful costumes, including Bavarian dirndl (full, gathered) skirts, and Austrian lederhosen (leather shorts). Some Teddylis had rubber bodies, which is unfortunate for collectors as rubber tends to crumble. The special edition Nimrod Teddy, produced in 1953 for the Steiff teddy bear's 50th birthday, is particularly sought after now. This 23cm (9in) bear was dressed as a huntsman, and came in four different colours wearing a felt tunic and cap and carrying a wooden rifle. Small Zotty bears also produced in the late 1960s, wore felt rompers or jackets with caps.

TEDDY BEAR PERSONALITIES

By the 1950s, a host of new teddy bear personalities was becoming popular through books, newspapers, comics, and the new medium of television. It was not long before children chose to dress their own bear in the costume of their favourite character. The television provided plenty of ideas. In Britain, the popular magazine programme, *Blue Peter*, which had been running since 1958, demonstrated many inventive ideas on how to dress your teddy bear. The accompanying book is still proving useful for many of today's teddy bear collectors.

△ **Flower Power**
Sophie, owned by British actress, Lisa Goddard, is very much a product of the 1960s. Her shape does not take conventional clothes, so she has flowers and a jacket embroidered onto her body instead.

◁ **Tank Top Ted**
Many teddy bear owners dress their bears in the fashion of the time. This bear's tank top dates him to the late 1960s.

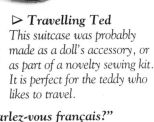

▷ **Travelling Ted**
This suitcase was probably made as a doll's accessory, or as part of a novelty sewing kit. It is perfect for the teddy who likes to travel.

◁ **"Parlez-vous français?"**
A bear dressed as a Frenchman, with a blue beret, blue and white striped top, and blue dungarees. His brilliant red bow and Eiffel tower brooch complete his outfit.

BEAR MEMORABILIA

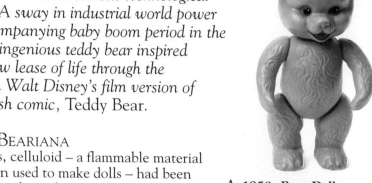

The era following the difficult days of World War II dawned with various technological advances and the arrival of new synthetic materials. A sway in industrial world power towards the Far East – Japan, in particular – and the accompanying baby boom period in the West, resulted in numerous cheaply made, colourful, and ingenious teddy bear inspired novelties. At the same time, the teddy bear was given a new lease of life through the emergence of comic strip characters, such as Baloo Bear in Walt Disney's film version of Kipling's The Jungle Book, and through the popular British comic, Teddy Bear.

SYNTHETIC BEARIANA

By the 1960s, celluloid – a flammable material that had been used to make dolls – had been officially banned as a dangerous substance and toy manufacturers resorted to soft or hard vinyl, which was relatively cheap and easy to mould into teddy bears. British firms, such as Rosebud, and Rodnoid, made straightforward, jointed copies of the traditional bear. Other firms, including Dunbee and Casdon, made squeaker toys, push-alongs, money boxes and toothbrush holders. Rubber versions of Punkinhead, the Cheeky-like bear (see p.83) made by Merrythought for the Canadian market, were produced from 1948-1956. Japan also made mechanical bears in vast quantities from 1950-1970. The appeal of these popular bears lies in the often humorous, domestic themes that are portrayed, such as a mother feeding baby, a visit to the dentist, or the boss at the office. Sometimes, these toys have ingenious mechanisms that allow up to seven actions to take place, including eyes lighting up and the expulsion of water.

△ **1950s Bear Doll**
A hard plastic, jointed doll made by Rosebud Dolls.

◁ **Book-worm Bear**
A 1950s Japanese bear with a clockwork mechanism and a magnet that makes his arm flick through the pages.

▷ **Russian Bear**
This Russian clockwork bear repeatedly raises his arm to lick his ice cream, while, at the same time, turning around on the spot.

△ **Glove Puppet**
One of the original Sooty glove puppets used in Harry Corbett's performances on British television and in the theatre.

TELEVISION TEDDIES

From the early 1950s, new teddy bear characters were introduced through the medium of television that had become a way of life in many homes. Many are now popular with collectors. Sooty, created by an English electrical engineer and amateur magician, Harry Corbett, made his debut on British television with his squeaky dog friend, Sweep, in 1952. Several companies produced related items. Chad Valley were given sole rights to reproduce the glove puppet, now a collector's item, especially if complete with a wooden wand. Since 1980, however, the puppets have been made in Taiwan and distributed by Patsy B. Marketing. Sooty fans have their own club and museum, based near Harry Corbett's home, and the show continues today in the hands of his son, Matthew. Perhaps the most famous animated bears brought into millions of homes world-wide in the 1960s were Yogi Bear, named after an American baseball player, and his friends, Boo Boo and Cindy. They were the creation of the American cartoon film makers, Hanna-Barbera.

△ **The Three Bears**
These three plastic bears with painted clothes date from the 1950s.

Merchandising soon included soft toys, such as those made by Merrythought. Australia has its own ursine television personality, Humphrey B. Bear who first appeared in a programme for pre-school children in the early 1960s. Classic Toys created their own Humphrey B. Bear who wears a tartan waistcoat and a boater – he is now particularly collectable. Other firms made related products, such as plastic versions of Humphrey B. Bear, and printed cloth covered in images of him.

▷ **Rattle**
A 1950s Japanese, synthetic plush bear in the shape of a child's rattle. His bulbous pantaloons contain jingling bells.

△ **Purse**
A 1940s teddy bear that doubles up as a money purse with an oilcloth lining. It looks fairly worn out and had probably been a favourite of its young owner. The purse is, perhaps, a forerunner of the teddy bear rucksack that became popular in the 1980s.

◁ **Teddy's Playtime**
This bone china mug dates from the 1960s. It has a Royal Albert design called Teddy's Playtime. Ceramic ware was also decorated with teddy bear characters.

❧ "Horst" ☙

1953 GEBRUDER HERMANN

This little bear was made at the new Hermann factory in Hirschaid, in the American Zone of Germany. The company relocated in 1948 and was run by Bernhard Hermann's three sons. Hermann bears continued to rival those from the Steiff factory: the one here is often confused with the Steiff Zotty, also introduced in the 1950s.

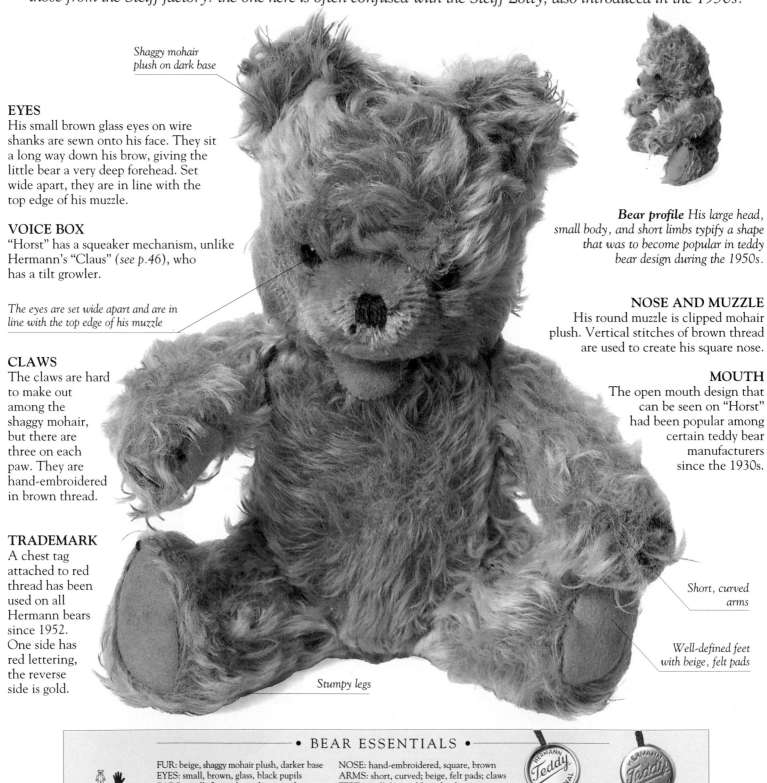

Shaggy mohair plush on dark base

EYES

His small brown glass eyes on wire shanks are sewn onto his face. They sit a long way down his brow, giving the little bear a very deep forehead. Set wide apart, they are in line with the top edge of his muzzle.

VOICE BOX

"Horst" has a squeaker mechanism, unlike Hermann's "Claus" (*see p.46*), who has a tilt growler.

The eyes are set wide apart and are in line with the top edge of his muzzle

CLAWS

The claws are hard to make out among the shaggy mohair, but there are three on each paw. They are hand-embroidered in brown thread.

TRADEMARK

A chest tag attached to red thread has been used on all Hermann bears since 1952. One side has red lettering, the reverse side is gold.

Bear profile His large head, small body, and short limbs typify a shape that was to become popular in teddy bear design during the 1950s.

NOSE AND MUZZLE

His round muzzle is clipped mohair plush. Vertical stitches of brown thread are used to create his square nose.

MOUTH

The open mouth design that can be seen on "Horst" had been popular among certain teddy bear manufacturers since the 1930s.

Short, curved arms

Well-defined feet with beige, felt pads

Stumpy legs

• BEAR ESSENTIALS •

HT: 25cm (10in)

FUR: beige, shaggy mohair plush, darker base
EYES: small, brown, glass, black pupils
EARS: small, flat and standing upright
MUZZLE: clipped mohair plush, protruding

NOSE: hand-embroidered, square, brown
ARMS: short, curved; beige, felt pads; claws
FEET: small; beige, felt pads; claws
STUFFING: wood-wool throughout bear

Trademark

❧ "Ross" ❧

c.1950 BRITISH

"Ross" is typical of British bears made in the 1940s and early 1950s, but he has one distinctive feature: his mouth can be opened and closed, using a lever at the back of his head. Other bears had mouths that you worked by pressing the stomach, by tipping the head back, or by pulling a ring located in the back of the bear's neck.

EARS
"Ross" has wide, flat ears, centred over the seams of his face. Much of the mohair plush has worn away.

Short, blunt muzzle

MOUTH
Two pieces of hinged hardboard in his mouth extend into the back of his head, where the ends are held apart by a large spring, covered with gauze. Two metal rods, connected to the hardboard, poke out from the back of the bear's head, where they are each tipped with a round ball of amber glass.

Pink, felt-lined mouth

STUFFING
"Ross" is stuffed with cotton waste wadding and some shredded stockingette. He has wood-wool packing around his internal mouth mechanism.

ARMS
The arms are short and relatively straight, with Rexine paw pads. These are now well worn.

His small feet are typical of British bears of this period

Amber eyes attached to long wire shanks

Bear profile *This side view clearly shows the levers in the back of his head, used to open and close his mouth.*

EYES
The ends of the threads holding the large glass eyes are fastened at the back of his head. Some glue has also been used behind the eyes to make them extra secure. Their bulbous nature is slightly reminiscent of the eyes on Merrythought's bear, "Colin" (see p.54).

NOSE
The nose at the end of his small, pointed muzzle consists of a rectangular piece of black felt, tightly bound with the original black thread, which has faded with age.

Damaged paw reveals cotton waste wadding

• BEAR ESSENTIALS •

HT: 37cm (14in)

FUR: pale golden-coloured, mohair plush
EYES: large, amber, glass, black pupils
EARS: wide, flat, centred over seams of face
MUZZLE: short, blunt; mouth opened by rods

NOSE: wide, rectangular, black felt, thread
ARMS: short; brown, Rexine pads; no claws
FEET: small; brown, Rexine pads; no claws
STUFFING: cotton wadding; wood-wool

DISTINGUISHING FEATURES: The short, straight arms, small feet, and low grade stuffing help identify "Ross" as a post-war British bear.

❧ Jackie-Baby ❧

1953 STEIFF

Jackie-Baby – the Jubilee bear – was produced to celebrate the Steiff teddy bear's 50th birthday. He was designed as a bear cub and was sold in three sizes with an accompanying booklet about the history of the firm. Replicas (also in three sizes) were produced by Steiff in 1986, 1989, and 1990.

EARS
Jackie-Baby has large, rounded ears placed along the top and sides of his head.

EYES
He has brown, glass eyes on wire shanks, sewn fairly wide apart along the top edge of the muzzle.

TRADEMARK
Jackie-Baby has a 1950s Steiff button, and a printed label bearing the manufacturer's name and "US Zone Germany" stitched into his side seam.

FEET
His feet are similar to those belonging to Merrythought's Bingie (*see p.55*) who is also a bear cub.

Damaged paw reveals wood-wool stuffing

Bear profile Notice Jackie-Baby's large head, with its protruding muzzle. His arms are long in comparison with his stumpy feet.

NOSE
Jackie-Baby's nose is particularly unusual: a horizontal pink stitch runs across the vertical stitches of dark brown thread.

FUR
Jackie-Baby is made of beige mohair plush; he has a distinct muzzle of clipped plush.

The small, dark area represents his navel

• BEAR ESSENTIALS •

HT: 38cm (15in)

FUR: beige, mohair plush; some clipped
EYES: small, brown, glass, wide apart
EARS: rounded, flat, on top and side of head
MUZZLE: large, protruding, clipped plush

NOSE: square; pink and brown stitches
ARMS: long; beige, felt pads; claws
FEET: large; beige, felt pads; no claws
STUFFING: wood-wool throughout bear

Trademark

New style, raised lettering

❧ "Felix" ❧

LATE 1950s DEAN'S RAG BOOK CO. LTD.

"Felix" was the creation of Sylvia R. Wilgoss, chief designer for Dean's from about 1950 until the late 1970s. Part of her successful Tru-to-Life series, this black bear was manufactured in three sizes at the Rye factory in Sussex, England. The company moved from Surrey to Sussex in 1956.

HEAD
His muzzle contrasts with the black plush used for his body. An underlying rubber mask forms the eye sockets, nose, and mouth.

Rubber eye sockets

EYES
The eyes are placed inside rubber sockets, which have been cut into the internal rubber face mask.

VOICE BOX
"Felix" has a tilt growler that still works.

LEGS
The unjointed legs are stuffed with wood-wool, and sewn to the front of his body. As a result, the bear is permanently sitting, like Merrythought's Bingie (*see p.55*).

TRADEMARK
A printed label is sewn into his back seam.

Ears set wide apart on sides of head

Bear profile *"Felix" has a large, realistic head, similar to the heads of the early, life-like Steiff bears.*

White plush muzzle

NOSE AND MOUTH
His large black nose and mouth, made of moulded rubber, protrude through the end of his white muzzle. Moulded rubber was used by Dean's for many of their noses.

ARMS
This bear's long, unjointed, soft-filled arms hang loosely at the side of his body. They are particularly floppy because of the lack of stuffing in his shoulders.

CLAWS
His feet pads and his paws are made of pink rubber, moulded into five claws. Some of the claws have become bent and damaged.

Life-like, flesh-coloured feet

• BEAR ESSENTIALS •

HT: 47cm (19in)

FUR: black-coloured, shaggy, acrylic plush
EYES: large, brown glass in rubber sockets
EARS: large, rounded, wide apart in seams
MUZZLE: white acrylic plush

NOSE: moulded rubber, large, protruding
ARMS: long; moulded rubber pads; claws
FEET: large; moulded rubber pads; claws
STUFFING: wood-wool and kapok

MADE IN ENGLAND by Dean's Rag Book CO. LTD LONDON

Trademark

❧ "Geoffrey" ❧
1955 CHAD VALLEY

"Geoffrey" was manufactured during a period of expansion for this already successful, British company: in 1938 it had received the Royal Warrant of Appointment from Her Majesty Queen Elizabeth (mother to Queen Elizabeth II). Originally a family business, Chad Valley became a public company in 1950.

EARS
The bear's wide, flat ears occupy the corners of his head, and are set more on the side of his head than the top.

VOICE BOX
When you tilt the bear, the voice box still works, emitting quite a high-pitched growl.

The curved arms taper at the shoulders and the paws

FUR
"Geoffrey" has an interesting coat of mixed brown and beige, shaggy mohair plush. The woven backing has a contrasting dark and light weft and warp.

FEET
His feet are small, and the ankles are not very clearly defined.

Bear profile He has a slightly protruding, but blunt, muzzle and a straight back. Notice how his legs are the same length as his arms.

Amber glass eyes, with black pupils

NOSE
His long, rectangular nose is typical of the noses on Chad Valley bears. It is composed mainly of vertical stitches.

Hand-embroidered, black thread mouth

TRADEMARK
A printed label on the left foot bears the Royal Warrant. Before 1953 it referred to "Queen Elizabeth"; after 1953 it changed to "Queen Mother", a point that helps with dating.

Mid-brown Rexine, or oilcloth, foot pads

• BEAR ESSENTIALS •

HT: 40cm (16in)

FUR: brown and beige, shaggy, mohair plush
EYES: medium, amber glass, black pupils
EARS: large, flat, located on side of head
MUZZLE: blunt and slightly protruding

NOSE: hand-embroidered, rectangular, black
ARMS: curved; brown, Rexine pads; claws
FEET: small; brown, Rexine pads; claws
STUFFING: kapok throughout bear

Royal warrant

Trademark

❧ *Cheeky* ❧

*c.*1960 MERRYTHOUGHT

Merrythought's endearing Cheeky design was first registered in 1957. It was produced in a variety of sizes and materials, always with a bell in each of the uniquely large ears. Dressed and open-mouthed Cheekies were also made, as well as Mr and Mrs Twisty Cheeky, a dressed couple (see pp.74-75).

EARS
Cheeky's large ears are sewn onto the sides of his head. The front of each ear is made from a darker nylon plush than the back. A metal bell is sandwiched between each piece of fabric.

EYES
Cheeky has large, plastic, lock-in eyes, a feature that became common in the late 1950s and 1960s *(see pp.72-73).* The original swing tag would have advertised these safe eyes.

MUZZLE
Cheeky's soft, squashy, velveteen muzzle is London-gold, a term used by Merrythought to describe its colour.

FEET
His feet are large and extremely wide. The pile on the brown, felt pads is slightly worn.

A label bearing the Merrythought trademark is stitched to his foot pad

Bear profile *Cheeky's large, domed head and pert nose are clear from this angle. Notice how his wide, cheeky smile extends right across the muzzle.*

Curly, honey-coloured nylon plush

NOSE AND MOUTH
The tip of the muzzle is tightly bound with black thread to suggest the nose. A cheeky grin embroidered underneath the nose gives the bear his name.

ARMS
Cheeky's curved arms are short. His shoulders are narrower than his wide, round paws.

The brown, felt pads on the paws are circular – an unusual shape

CLAWS
Five relatively short claws are stitched in black thread on each of the foot and paw pads.

• BEAR ESSENTIALS •

HT: 38cm (15in)

FUR: honey-coloured, curly, nylon plush
EYES: amber, safe, plastic, black pupils
EARS: large, placed on sides of head
MUZZLE: small, pointed, golden velveteen

NOSE: hand-embroidered, triangular, black
ARMS: wide, round; circular, felt pads; claws
FEET: large, wide; brown, felt pads; claws
STUFFING: kapok throughout bear

Trademark

❧ "Cully" ❧

c.1963 WENDY BOSTON PLAYSAFE TOYS LTD.

"Cully" is an excellent example of a machine-washable teddy bear, made from all-synthetic materials. The idea was first introduced by the Wendy Boston firm in 1954. A quarter of the teddy bears exported from Britain came from their Welsh factory, until its take-over by Denys Fisher in 1968.

"Cully's" wide ears are from the same piece of fabric as his head

EYES
"Cully" boasts the famous nylon screw-locked eyes, patented by Ken and Wendy (*née* Boston) Williams in 1948. They consist of an outer ring of amber-coloured plastic, and a black pupil made of a moulded, nylon screw and bolt.

Black thread binds the end of his nose

Bear profile *"Cully" is unjointed and has a fairly flat body, representing a departure from the traditional teddy bear design.*

Each paw has three claws of black thread

STUFFING
The plastic foam stuffing, a soft and washable material that revolutionized the soft toy industry when it was first introduced, has since proved highly toxic if set on fire. It also deteriorates with time.

ARMS
The unjointed arms are short and curved. The way they are attached to his body makes them stretch out in an endearing expression of love.

Shaggy, nylon woven plush

LEGS
"Cully" has no clearly defined feet. His legs are straight and stocky, with oval pads of short pile plush on the ends.

FUR
"Cully" is made from shaggy nylon plush on a woven backing. A short-piled nylon plush is used on his muzzle, foot pads, and paws.

Satin label stitched on right pad

• BEAR ESSENTIALS •

HT: 55cm (22in)

FUR: honey and black, woven-nylon plush
EYES: amber, safe, nylon, black pupils
EARS: large, wide, flat, part of head
MUZZLE: large, short, nylon plush

NOSE: hand-stitched, rectangular, black
ARMS: curved; honey-coloured pads; claws
FEET: formless; short pile pads; no claws
STUFFING: shredded plastic foam

WENDY BOSTON
Made in England
Wash in luke-warm suds

Trademark

❧ "Bobby Bear" ❧

c.1955 PEDIGREE SOFT TOYS LTD.

Pedigree Soft Toys was a subsidiary of Lines Brothers Ltd., once Britain's largest and most successful toy company. The firm started manufacturing bears in 1937 at Lines' Tri-ang Works in Merton, Surrey; they registered their trademark in 1942. "Bobby Bear" was made at Pedigree's Belfast factory, which opened in 1946.

EARS
The inner edges of each flat ear are folded over, then the whole ear is sewn into the horizontal seam running along the top of the bear's head.

EYES
His plastic eyes are early examples of the safe, lock-in type. A washer behind the fabric probably holds them in place. The amber and black parts appear to be fused together, differentiating them from a Wendy Boston bear's eyes (see p.84).

"Bobby Bear's" red bow is a later embellishment

VOICE BOX
You can feel the remains of a squeaker inside "Bobby Bear's" narrow, wood-wool filled body. It no longer works, though.

The golden mohair plush is well worn

FEET
There is only a slight indication of rounded feet at the ends of the virtually straight, plump legs.

Almost circular pads of beige velveteen show signs of wear and tear

Bear profile At this angle, it is possible to see "Bobby Bear's" very rounded head, which only has a slight indication of a muzzle. His thin torso, short, straight limbs, and lack of feet are a definite departure from the traditional teddy bear shape.

Black thread mouth

NOSE
The square-shaped nose is made up of vertical stitches in black thread binding the end of the bear's particularly blunt muzzle.

ARMS
"Bobby Bear's" arms are short and almost straight – they are just slightly curved towards his clawless paws.

STUFFING
"Bobby Bear's" head and body are stuffed with wood-wool; his limbs are filled with kapok.

Little remains of the bear's velveteen paw pads

TRADEMARK
A printed, fabric label is stitched into "Bobby Bear's" back seam.

• BEAR ESSENTIALS •

HT: 45cm (18in)

FUR: golden-coloured, mohair plush
EYES: amber, safe, plastic, black pupils
EARS: medium, flat, edge folded over
MUZZLE: only slightly distinguishable

NOSE: hand-embroidered, square, black
ARMS: curved; velveteen pads; no claws
FEET: barely exist; velveteen pads; no claws
STUFFING: wood-wool and kapok mixture

PADDINGTON BEAR

Paddington Bear from Darkest Peru, with his penchant for marmalade, his duffle coat, and his humorous attempts as a kindly but accident-prone foreigner trying to understand the British way of life, has universal appeal. He shot to fame in 1958 when Michael Bond's book, A Bear Called Paddington, was published. The book was a resounding success, and so from 1960 onwards Michael Bond's stories were published in the United States and translated into numerous languages. In Japan, Paddington features on the credit card of the Mitsui Bank.

△ **Bear Boots**
Paddington boots

THE RISE OF PADDINGTON

Michael Bond based the character on a teddy bear he had bought for his wife from the London store, Selfridges, in 1956. The bear was later given a duffle coat, hat, and suitcase. He had a book a year published up until 1966, and then six new collections of Paddington stories followed between 1968 and 1981. Paperbacks came soon after the hardbacks, along with novelties such as pop-up, birthday, and picture books for young readers. Peggy Fortnum's delightful illustrations contributed to the early Paddington's popularity, although other artists such as Fred Banberry, David McKee, and Ivor Wood, have also portrayed the bear. Barry Macey illustrated Paddington's 25th birthday book written specially for Selfridges in 1983.

WORLD-WIDE APPEAL

Paddington Bear stories featured on British radio and television in the 1960s, and the first musical based on his adventures was performed in both Britain and Australia in 1973. It was the animated puppet series originally shown on British television in 1975, however, that contributed to the bear's wider following. This was sold to nearly every country in the world, and was an international success.

△ **Paddington Man**
Michael Bond, the creator of Paddington Bear, with some of the original illustrations from his books.

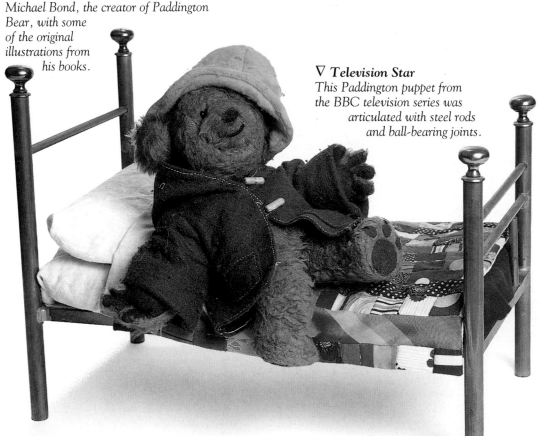

▽ **Television Star**
This Paddington puppet from the BBC television series was articulated with steel rods and ball-bearing joints.

△ **Book Illustrations**
Paddington, as drawn by Peggy Fortnum.

△ **Pair of Slippers**
Paddington foot-wear.

EARLY MERCHANDISING

Paddington wallpaper was available from 1967, but it was not until the 1970s that the merchandising of this bear really expanded. One of the earliest Paddington licensees was Gabrielle Designs, producers of the first soft toy Paddington in Britain in 1972; since 1975, New York-based Eden Toys Inc. have held the licence for manufacturing soft toy Paddingtons throughout the rest of the world. Their bear differed from the British Paddington, in that he had no safety pin in his hat; a pin would have contravened American safety regulations.

FROM BOARD GAMES TO BICYCLE BELLS

Paddington's popularity was so considerable that Michael Bond went on to form "Paddington and Co.". They were responsible for monitoring the licensing of hundreds of products, ranging from Paddington board games to bicycle bells, and from chocolate to cassettes. In 1978, a shop, "Paddington and Friends", was opened in London, dedicated to the internationally famous literary character. A permanent display of Paddington memorabilia can be seen at the London Toy and Model Museum, near Paddington Station in London. On the concourse of the station, a large bear called Paddington has stood since 1978.

△ **Learning with Paddington**
Paddington enjoying his "elevenses" – the British colloquial term for a mid-morning snack. His books are used abroad, to help teach English customs and expressions.

Bear in Boots
Shirley Clarkson, of Gabrielle Designs, gave Paddington a pair of Wellington Boots. Michael Bond later wrote these accessories into the stories. The boots have paw marks and PB written in reverse on the soles.

△ **Paddington's Aunt Lucy**
Gabrielle Designs also created a bear called Aunt Lucy. According to Paddington lore, Aunt Lucy had looked after the young Paddington before his journey to England. She wears traditional Peruvian clothes, including a bowler hat.

❧ "Joycie" ☙

c.1960 JOY TOYS

"Joycie" was made by one of Australia's earliest teddy bear manufacturers. The firm was established by Gerald Kirby and his wife in Melbourne during the late 1920s. A flourishing company making a wide range of soft toys, Joy Toys was taken over by the British Lines Brothers' firm in 1966, and eventually disbanded in the late 1970s.

EARS
"Joycie" has small, rounded ears placed squarely over the seams of her face. They are stitched into a seam running along the top of her head.

EYES
Her attractive, blue glass eyes have metal shanks secured with strong cotton. The cotton is fastened off in the middle of her head, at the back.

VOICE BOX
"Joycie" has a squeaker mechanism imported from West Germany. It consists of a round spring, encased in soft, clear vinyl; a harder, clear vinyl top contains the reed. The voice box is pushed into a hole cut in the bear's filling.

FEET
The bear's legs are straight and unjointed. Half-circular pieces of mohair plush form the top of her prominent feet.

Oval foot pads are made from the same pale pink, synthetic, knitted plush as the body

Her muzzle protrudes slightly, and is blunt at the end

Bear profile *The flatness of "Joycie's" completely unjointed body, particularly her all-in-one torso and legs, is very evident from this angle.*

Black thread mouth

NOSE
The square nose consists of several vertical stitches of black thread.

Arms point upwards very slightly

ARMS
The short, unjointed arms are stitched to the sides of the body, and are outstretched in an endearing manner. No paws are indicated.

STUFFING
This Australian bear is made of plastic foam filling, specially moulded to fit into the knitted plush skin.

TRADEMARK
A printed label, with the manufacturer's name, is folded and sewn into the inside seam of the bear's right leg.

• BEAR ESSENTIALS •

HT: 31cm (12in)

FUR: pale pink, synthetic knitted plush
EYES: medium-sized, blue, glass, black pupils
EARS: small, rounded, square over face seams
MUZZLE: blunt and slightly protruding

NOSE: hand-embroidered, square, black
ARMS: no paws indicated; no pads; no claws
FEET: prominent; plush pads, no claws
STUFFING: plastic foam cut to body shape

JOY-TOYS
MADE IN AUSTRALIA
Trademark

❧ "Leon" ❧

1962 H.G. STONE & CO. LTD.

"Leon", another Hugmee bear (see p.67), was manufactured at H.G. Stone's Pontypool factory in Wales. He was made prior to the death of his namesake, Leon Rees, one of the company's founders. In 1964, H.G. Stone was taken over by Dunbee-Combex-Marx, a British company, manufacturing vinyl dolls and toys.

VOICE BOX
You can feel a round squeaker, probably of the kind that uses card, a spring, and oilcloth (*see p.73*), inside "Leon's" rounded body. It is still working.

Amber and black plastic, safe, lock-in eyes

FEET
"Leon's" large feet have long, pointed, velveteen pads, reinforced with card. Similar Chiltern bears with Rexine pads date from an earlier period.

Despite H.G. Stone's move to Pontypool, the company still maintained the Chiltern name for their bears

TRADEMARK
A printed label is stitched to "Leon's" left side seam under his arm. He also has a printed card swing tag, noting that he was: "Awarded the Certificate of the Royal Institute of Public Health and Hygiene".

Honey-coloured mohair plush

Thin, black, embroidery-silk mouth

Bear profile *From the side, you can see "Leon's" typical, Chiltern, flat-backed head, with its extensive forehead and slightly protruding muzzle.*

NOSE
The shape of "Leon's" small nose resembles a heraldic shield. The nose consists of vertical stitches of thin, black, embroidery silk. Chiltern bears of this period also had moulded plastic noses, although the company finally reverted back to stitching, preferring the traditional method.

ARMS
The arms are longer than the legs, but are tapered, with very wide shoulders. They are curved in the usual way.

CLAWS
"Leon" has five claws stitched on the plush of each foot. He has only four claws on his paws. These run from the pad onto the plush.

The thread used for the claws is double thickness

• BEAR ESSENTIALS •

HT: 53cm (21in)

FUR: honey-coloured, mohair plush
EYES: amber, safe, plastic, black pupils
EARS: long, narrow, gathered at base
MUZZLE: blunt, slightly protruding, rounded

NOSE: hand-stitched, shield-like, black
ARMS: curved; long, beige pads; claws
FEET: large; reinforced, velveteen pads; claws
STUFFING: kapok and wood-wool

THE TEDDY COMES OF AGE

Anumber of people and events at the end of the 1960s and early 1970s were to have a lasting impact on the development of the teddy bear. The publication of The Teddy Bear Book by the British actor, Peter Bull, in 1969, was the main precursor of what was to become an international arctophily movement. The book not only surveyed, almost for the first time, the teddy bear's history – his origins and the developments of the teddy bear manufacturing industry – but also considered the toy's unique relationship with his or her owner and the significance in that person's life.

THE TEDDY BEAR RENAISSANCE

The new awareness of bears was further fuelled by the various teddy bear books and events coming out of the "International Year of the Child" in 1979. Together with the work of "Good Bears of the World", an organization providing needy children with teddy bears, they succeeded in bringing together many like-minded people. The era experienced a teddy bear renaissance, a mania similar to that of the early years. This time, however, it was more remarkable because of multi-media coverage and technological advancements.

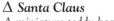

△ Santa Claus
A miniature teddy bear dressed as Santa Claus, made by American bear artist, Linda Kuch.

CHANGING HANDS

The new wave of nostalgia, the public's greater awareness of their heritage and the value of craftsmanship, encouraged the establishment of cottage industries, producing handmade, traditionally designed teddy bears from a combination of natural and modern materials. The worldwide economic recession of the 1970s led to the downfall of many of the major teddy bear manufacturers by the 1980s. For example, products belonging to the British firm Palitoy, who owned the Chad Valley label, and Pedigree Soft Toys Ltd., were lost to the American Hasbro, originally the Hassenfield Brothers Inc., who were destined to become world leaders in the toy field. Such multi-national companies now play an important role in teddy manufacture.

▽ Peter Bull
Actor, Peter Bull, was also author of The Teddy Bear Book *and A Hug of Teddy Bears.*

△ Hands
Applause was once a division of the famous Knickerbocker Toy Co..

△ Bear Artist
The trademark of well-known American bear artist, Mac Pohlen, based in California.

NEW STANDARD OF SAFETY

Regulations regarding the physical, flammable, and toxicological properties of toys were constantly updated. In 1978, Britain brought their safety standards into line with other European countries. In 1989, the Lion mark was introduced to indicate to shoppers which toys conformed to current British standards. Despite the earlier breakthrough on bear washability, many teddies were made carrying instructions to "surface wash only".

△ Bejewelled Bear
The romantic author, Barbara Cartland, once owned this bear, now at the Teddy Bear Museum in Stratford-upon-Avon, England.

TEDDY BEAR ARTISTS

The late 1970s saw a number of individuals setting themselves up as teddy bear artists, a phenomenon at first peculiar to the United States, although it spread world-wide during the 1980s. The forerunners of this movement include names such as Dee Hockenberry (*see p.113*), Beverly Wright, Flore Emory, and Doris and Terry Michaud. These artists designed and hand-made bears, often based on the traditional style, in limited editions. Several artists chose to exaggerate the basic form. Ballard Baines and Linda Spiegel, for example, made rather unnatural looking creatures with thin, bent limbs. Other artists used untraditional materials: in the United States, Beverly Port designs porcelain-faced bears, while the creations of Robert Raikes have wooden faces (*see p.109*).

IMAGINATIONS RUN WILD

Some of the larger firms began to use unconventional fabrics. The North-American Bear Co.'s brightly coloured VIB's (*see pp.94-95*) or Gabrielle Designs' terry towelling bears, are examples. Imaginations began to run wild as numerous personalities, vampires, red Indian squaws, Santa Claus, and Santa Lucia themes were applied to the modern bear. The ultimate of these bears are the bears in disguise, such as Bev Miller's Bunny Bear, while Flore Emory and Ginger T. Brame have produced Bumble Bears, with striped plush bodies, wings and antennae. Teddy bears had reached art form status when Kimberlee Port's plush Christmas Tree Bear covered in decorations, was exhibited in a New York gallery in 1987.

LUXURY ITEMS

These sophisticated personality bears were produced for adults, rather than children. They were designed as a luxury accessory, the ultimate example being the expensive mink teddy bear available at London's Fortnum and Mason store in 1980. Some bears are designed as collector's pieces, and capture the elongated features of the earlier teddy designs. The bears of Naomi Laight (*see p.108*), and Susan Rixon (*see p.111*) are cases in point. Some artists reverted to the use of traditional boot buttons, or glass eyes. If such eyes are used, the toys have a tag reading, "This is not a child's toy".

△ American Creation
This bear is the work of the American contemporary bear artist, Ginger T. Brame.

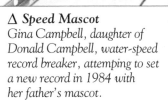

△ Speed Mascot
Gina Campbell, daughter of Donald Campbell, water-speed record breaker, attemping to set a new record in 1984 with her father's mascot.

◁ Oriental Accessory
A teddy bear paper garland made in Taiwan for the American market.

△ Teddy Socks
Today, teddy bears appear on all kinds of merchandise.

△ Happy Birthday
American bear artist, Bev Wright's teddies have their birthday written on card swing tags.

▽ American Artist's Work
The creations of some contemporary American bear artists.

BEAR NECESSITIES

I n recent years two types of teddy bears have emerged. Some manufacturers are making an unjointed, cuddly creature from safe, all-synthetic, fully-washable materials for children. Others aim for the collectors' market and, using natural materials such as mohair plush, make traditional jointed bears with long limbs, muzzles, and humped backs. Teddy bears that can walk and talk, with the help of microchips installed in their bodies, are also being produced.

JOINTS
Moulded, plastic, all-in-one discs and pins have been introduced.

Safe plastic eye with metal washer

NOSE
Plastic, moulded noses are either realistic or stylized. They are usually secured with a washer.

Plastic boot button eyes

BOOT BUTTON EYES
Replica, boot button eyes, copying the traditional designs on early bears, are secured with washers in the safe, modern way.

Plastic cover   *Metal washer*

PLASTIC EYES
Safe, lock-in, plastic eyes come in a wide variety of sizes and colours. They are held in place with metal washers which, occasionally, have additional plastic covers for extra security.

FABRIC
Teddies destined to be children's toys are made with artificial, plush fabrics. There is, nevertheless, a marked move towards natural fibres, like mohair, for bears aimed at the collectors' market. "Distressed" mohair, which is treated to appear old, was introduced in the mid-1980s.

Woven mohair plush

Half-mohair, half-wool, on cotton backing

Distressed mohair plush

Cotton thread   *Nylon thread*

MACHINE-STITCHING
The separate parts of a bear are machine-stitched together with cotton or synthetic thread. Clear nylon has become popular, being both strong and invisible.

Shredded plastic foam

Wood-wool

Acrylic plush on knitted backing

Plastic frame for small bear

MINI-BEARS
Tiny bears have moulded, plastic frames, with swivel-jointed limbs and heads.

DETAILS
Embroidery thread is still popular for the task of hand-stitching noses, mouths, and claws, but wool is also used.

Wool   *Embroidery thread*

Draylon
Synthetic plush

PAD FABRICS
Artificial fabrics, such as Draylon, are widely used, but the makers of traditional bears prefer real suede or chamois leather.

Coloured felts

Suedette

Suede

Japanese musical box with clear plastic lid

MUSICAL BOXES
Encased in plastic since the 1960s, the Swiss clockwork movement mechanism (*see p.37*) is now made by Japanese firms.

Plastic, flat squeaker

Plastic, concertina squeaker

Reed

Plastic tube for reed

TILT GROWLER
The weight and bellows are now contained in a plastic canister. The growl comes through a perforated speaker.

SQUEAKER
Squeakers are made of thin, moulded plastic and are either flat or a concertina shape. Both have metal and plastic reeds, protected by a plastic tube.

Perforated speaker

Polyester wadding

1988 APPLAUSE
Made in California, this unjointed bear is filled with polyester stuffing. His plush is artificial, he has lock-in plastic, replica boot button eyes, a lock-in plastic nose and a stitched mouth.

Plastic foam and polystyrene pellet mix

Low-grade cotton waste

STUFFING
Wood-wool is favoured, particularly for the heads of collectors' bears. As plastic foam pieces and polystyrene pellets used in the 1950s and 1960s were found to crumble, and to give off toxic fumes in the event of fire, polyester wadding came into its own in the 1970s. Low-grade cotton waste is still used for cheap bears.

BEAR APPAREL

With the advent of arctophily, and the return of the traditional, jointed, teddy-doll shape in the 1970s, bears with wardrobes full of clothes came back into fashion. The inventiveness that had been lacking since before World War II returned with a vengeance as each manufacturer tried to tempt the collector with yet another bear in disguise. Teddy bears, it seemed, could no longer remain just bare bears. They had to be employed in every kind of occupation that could give rise to an outfit easily worn by an upright, furry animal. In the United States, in particular, the imagination of some manufacturers ran wild. These designer bears are, however, for the affluent buyer.

△ **Biggles Bear**
An airport souvenir made in the 1980s.

UNIFORMED BEARS

The 1970s were difficult years for the toy industry yet, despite this, several manufacturers produced curious novelty bears in costume. Steiff's 1972 Hockey Teddy had a numbered, blue plush jersey, which was all-in-one with his body and limbs. Merrythought continued the tradition of the masculine, uniformed teddy with their Beefeater, Policeman, Guardsman, and Highlander Bears. These were first produced in the early 1970s and they were later reintroduced in the 1980s. Meanwhile the 20th birthday of their successful Cheeky bear (*see p.83*) in 1977, was celebrated with the launch of Bedtime Bear, sporting pyjamas and a bright red dressing gown. The Chicago-based North-American Bear Co. made a range of famous historical figures, including Napoleon Bearnaparte and the Statue of Libearty. Sporting bears, such as Hermann's Golfer with his tartan plus fours and cap, and golfing trolley, were particularly popular. Bocs Teganau have made a bear dressed as Geoffrey Boycott, the famous British cricketer; he wears his full cricket kit, and holds a miniature V12 Slazenger bat.

◁ **Back to School**
This schoolboy bear with his leather satchel was made in a limited edition of 100 bears by the British company, Dormouse Designs, in 1989.

△ Sailor Bear
*A limited edition Bob Raikes
bear made in 1985.*

DESIGNER OUTFITS

As in the period of teddy bear mania at the beginning of the century, various manufacturers attempted to meet the growing demand for individual outfits. In the United States, the North-American Bear Co. produced the Vander Bear Family who came with a variety of outfits and accessories to which collectors could add, such as the Musical Soiree and the Victorian sleep-wear sets. In Britain, small firms followed suit. The Sussex-based Bear Wear Co., for example, produced limited edition, designer, hand-knitted sweaters and other unique outfits. A range of bears known as the Sloane Ranger Bears (named after a particular social elite who live around Sloane Square in London) was produced in England. These bears wore appropriate Sloane Ranger outfits, such as salopettes for skiing, and Barbour jackets for the country. British walkers were also parodied in the English Lakeland Bears series, wearing traditional walking gear and hand-made North Country clogs. However, as always, children today are still likely to practise their first hesitant "knit one, purl one" on teddy's new scarf or jumper, so there are still plenty of home-made clothes around.

△ Star Struck
*Humphrey Beargart was
made by the North-American
Bear Co..*

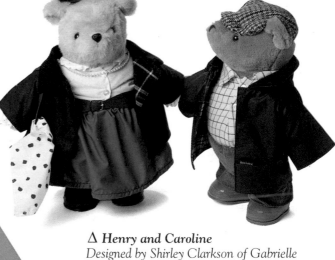

△ Henry and Caroline
*Designed by Shirley Clarkson of Gabrielle
Designs, Henry and Caroline are part
of her Sloane Ranger range
representing young upwardly mobile
professionals, known as yuppies.*

◁ Here Comes The Bride
*The lovely bridegroom and bride were
reproduced by Franklin Mint in the late
1980s. They are based on teddy bears in
the collection of the late Colonel Bob
Henderson (see p.122-123).*

BEAR MEMORABILIA

The teddy bear craze that had taken the world by storm at the beginning of the century, returned with renewed vigour in its latter years. Manufacturers competed with each other to fulfill the demands of the dedicated arctophile, providing him or her with every conceivable teddy-inspired accessory, from jewellery, ornaments, clothing, and household items, to fridge magnets, press button telephones, and car alarms. There was also renewed interest in the miniature bears, which had been common in the 1930s, and this was helped by the simultaneous rise in popularity of dolls' houses and miniature collecting. As a result of the technological advances in the electronics industry, several unique, talking bears appeared on the international market in the mid 1980s.

△ Teddy Lapel Pin
This pin was made in 1984 by Steiff.

TELEVISION STARS

The success of merchandising television characters like Paddington in the early 1970s *(see p.86-87)*, inspired others to follow suit. The most notable in the teddy bear world was Super Ted and, later, Tough Ted who were both originally characters in children's books. Tough Ted, created by Simon Bond, was an ex-Merchant Navy seabear, who ran a seaside café. After appearing on television, he was reproduced as a soft toy by Golden Bear Products, with a torn ear, five o'clock shadow, and embroidered tattoos.

◁ Super Ted
Super Ted – the creation of Mike Young – was originally a children's book character. He featured in a highly successful animated cartoon series, shown world-wide on television in the 1980s. This version was produced in the United States.

◁ Teddy in School
This little ted was made by the contemporary bear artist, Elaine Fujita-Gamble. He has his own desk, books, and an apple for his lunch.

▷ Teddy Ruxpin
First produced in 1984 by the large American toy company, Mattel, Teddy Ruxpin can talk with the aid of a story-telling cassette.

THE ULTIMATE BEAR GIMIC

Manufacturers are constantly striving to create the ultimate teddy bear novelty. The production of miniature teddy bears has become a serious art form. In the United States, artists such as Elaine Fujita-Gamble, Dickie Harrison, Linda Kuch, and Laurie Sasaki produce highly collectable miniature bears, while in Britain, the tiny teds of Anita Oliver, some only 2.5cm (1in) high, are prized. Each bear is traditionally jointed, hand sewn, and stuffed with kapok. Miniature teddy bears are also produced in ceramic, silver, pewter, crystal, and modern synthetic materials. Especially unusual are those made out of moss or fresh bread.

The ultimate is, perhaps, Mr Bills, produced in 1987 from clear polythene, and stuffed with a quarter of a million shredded dollar notes. With the development of the microchip, manufacturers attempted to create a teddy bear with a realistic speaking mechanism. Hasbro's Bingo Bear has a 400-word vocabulary, revealed when he is cuddled or his chin is scratched. Mattel's Teddy Ruxpin blinks, wriggles his nose, and opens and shuts his mouth in perfect synchronization with his voice, which is in the form of story-telling cassette.

△ Ted-in-the-Box
This tiny ted is only the size of a postage stamp.

△ Muff and Purse Bear
This muff and purse bear was made by Merrythought in the 1980s.

▽ Bear Chair
A child's chair made of pine by the British firm, Bear Essentials.

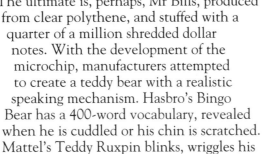

◁ Money Bear
Bear artist, Sue E. Foskey, made this money bear in 1987. When you put down the flap of the bag, the bear growls.

▷ Fozzie Bear
The original Fozzie Bear, now a museum piece in England, was designed by the late Jim Henson, creator of The Muppets.

❧ "Darren" ❧

1975 PEDIGREE SOFT TOYS LTD.

"Darren" was manufactured in Canterbury, England, where Pedigree was based throughout the 1970s and 1980s, until its eventual collapse in 1988. In 1966, the firm merged with Rovex Industries Ltd., a subsidiary of the Lines Brothers Group. Both companies were taken over by Dunbee-Combex-Marx in 1972.

EARS
The bear's very large ears are flat and narrow. They are sewn more onto the sides than onto the top of his large head.

EYES
His safe, lock-in eyes are made of amber and black plastic, and they are positioned just inside each face seam.

VOICE BOX
"Darren's" rounded body houses a modern plastic tilt growler. The original box in which he was bought advertised, "I growl".

Thin, black, stitched mouth

FEET
The stumpy feet have irregularly shaped oval pads made from dark brown, synthetic velvet. There is no indication of claws.

TRADEMARK
A printed, satin label bearing the manufacturer's name is folded over, and stitched into the lower part of the bear's back seam.

Bear profile *At this angle, the bear's large head and ears, his small, rounded, slightly protruding muzzle, and short, stumpy limbs are clear.*

Clipped nylon plush with a woven backing

NOSE
"Darren" has a moulded, black plastic nose, slightly reminiscent of a dog's. It is secured on the end of his muzzle with a washer.

The ribbon is original

ARMS
The upward curving arms are the same length as the legs. They are wider in the centres than at the shoulders and paws.

Golden-coloured flame-resistant plush with a knitted backing

❧ BEAR ESSENTIALS ❧

HT: 40cm (16in)

FUR: golden, flame-resistant nylon plush
EYES: amber, safe, plastic, black pupils
EARS: large, wide, flat, on sides of head
MUZZLE: protruding, clipped nylon plush

NOSE: moulded plastic, dog-like, black
ARMS: short; brown, synthetic pads; no claws
FEET: stumpy; brown, synthetic pads; no claws
STUFFING: shredded plastic foam

✤ "Trayton" ✤

1976 MERRYTHOUGHT LTD.

Merrythought manufactured a series of traditional teddy bears from 1965 until 1985. They were made in nine sizes: this example, the smallest, was introduced in 1975. Before World War II all the plush came from mills in Yorkshire, England, but the mohair now used by Merrythought is largely imported, often from the Far East.

EYES
His small, amber and black plastic eyes are the safe lock-in type. They are set low down, giving him a high forehead, a feature typical of a later British bear.

ARMS
"Trayton's" short arms are tapered, with thin paws curving upwards. The synthetic pads are brown.

The mohair plush is a colour Merrythought describe as "London gold"

FEET
"Trayton's" very small feet are barely distinguishable from his legs. The brown, knitted, synthetic pads are irregular in shape.

Large, flat ears positioned across face seams

***Bear profile** "Trayton" is a typical, late British bear with a flat, rounded muzzle, arms and legs of the same length, almost non-existent feet, and a thin, straight body.*

An inverted V-shaped mouth

NOSE
The almost round nose is embroidered with black, mainly vertical stitches, with a few horizontal ones on top.

The flamboyant red bow is original

TRADEMARK
"Trayton" has a printed label on his right foot, and a printed card swing tag.

✤ BEAR ESSENTIALS ✤

HT: 25cm (10in)

FUR: London gold, pure mohair plush
EYES: amber, safe, plastic, black pupils
EARS: large, flat, squarely across face seams
MUZZLE: blunt, rounded, slightly protruding

NOSE: hand-embroidered, rounded, black
ARMS: short; synthetic pads; no claws
FEET: small; synthetic pads; no claws
STUFFING: kapok; wood-wool muzzle

Trademark

❧ "Brummy" ❧

1977 CHILTERN/CHAD VALLEY

In 1967, Chiltern Soft Toys became a subsidiary of Chad Valley, creating England's largest soft toy manufacturers. Ten years later, "Brummy" was produced in Birmingham. In 1978, Chad Valley was bought by the nearby Leicester firm, Palitoy, which in turn was taken over by the American company, Kenner Parker in the 1980s.

EARS
"Brummy's" large and rounded, flat ears are stitched squarely over his facial seams.

EYES
His plastic eyes are amber and black. They are the safe lock-in type used by most manufacturers of the time.

Slightly protruding muzzle

VOICE BOX
A red plastic, concertina squeaker (*see pp.92-93*) is embedded in "Brummy's" body.

Golden-coloured, luxury mohair plush

FEET
"Brummy's" small feet have tear-shaped pads of brown, knitted, synthetic material. He does not have any claws, a feature typical of British bears made in this period.

Bear profile This view reveals the flatness of his design, his thin body, small head, and his uniformly short limbs.

Black thread mouth

NOSE
"Brummy's" small, almost square nose is hand-stitched in black thread. It is more like the noses of early Chiltern teddies, than the easily recognizable, long, thick noses found on Chad Valley bears.

Original orange bow

TRADEMARK
The names, Chad Valley and Chiltern, are printed with the Royal Warrant on a card swing tag. The Royal Warrant was granted to Chad Valley in 1938.

ARMS
The bear's short arms are the same length as his legs. They have a slight curve, and the paw ends are hooked.

• BEAR ESSENTIALS •

HT: 30cm (12in)

FUR: golden-coloured, luxury mohair plush	NOSE: hand-embroidered, squarish, black
EYES: amber, safe, plastic, black pupils	ARMS: short; brown, synthetic pads; no claws
EARS: rounded, flat, squarely over face seams	FEET: small; brown, synthetic pads; no claws
MUZZLE: blunt and slightly protruding	STUFFING: coloured, synthetic fabric waste

Trademark

❧ *Bigo Bello* ❧
c.1970 SCHREYER & CO.

Bigo Bello was one of a Schuco series of plush toys, made to be bent into a variety of postures. This bear also talks when you pull a cord out from his side. The patented range was produced from the 1960s, before the firm was taken over in 1976 by Dunbee-Combex-Marx, one of Europe's leading toy manufacturers.

EARS
The bear's flat ears create a slight curve. They are placed squarely over the seams of his face.

EYES
The clear glass eyes with brown, painted backs and black pupils are typically Schuco. They are secured with hooked wire shanks.

VOICE BOX
Bigo Bello's wood-wool filled stomach contains a mechanism commonly used from the late 1950s. When you pull the cord at the side of the bear, a miniature record inside a protective plastic box plays eight German phrases. Translated, they include "Hello, Mummy", "My name is Bigo Bello", and "Give me a kiss".

Cream, clipped rayon plush pads with no claws

LIMBS
Bigo Bello is unjointed, but a flexible, wire armature in his limbs makes it possible to bend him into a variety of postures.

Long, brown artificial silk plush on a woven backing

Flexible, soft-filled legs and arms

Bear profile Bigo Bello has a rounded stomach, and straight, unjointed legs. From this angle, you can see the plastic ring that you pull to activate his voice.

Single black vertical stitch extending from nose to mouth

NOSE AND MUZZLE
His black nose is made from hard vinyl. It is glued to a muzzle made from the same clipped artificial silk plush as the foot and paw pads.

Printed card tag and cream ribbon attached to chest

MOUTH
This Schuco bear has an open mouth, similar to that of his older cousin, "Heinrich" (*see p.59*). Bigo Bello's mouth, however, is lined with flesh-coloured felt, and he has a tongue represented by a smudge of red paint. The edge of the jaw is defined by a thin line of brown paint.

• BEAR ESSENTIALS •

HT: 40cm (16in)

FUR: brown, long, artificial silk plush
EYES: medium, glass, brown painted backs
EARS: small, slightly curved, over face seams
MUZZLE: clipped artificial silk plush

NOSE: smooth, moulded vinyl, oval, black
ARMS: unjointed; cream pads; no claws
FEET: large; cream pads; no claws
STUFFING: wood-wool; soft-filled

Trademark

❧ Bully Bear ❧

1981 THE HOUSE OF NISBET LTD.

The House of Nisbet started off in 1953 as a doll-making business, but in 1978 it began making teddy bears for the collectors' market. Alison Wilson, daughter of the founder, designed Bully Bear for their Nisbet Childhood Classics range, drawing inspiration from a bear belonging to Peter Bull, late English actor and arctophile.

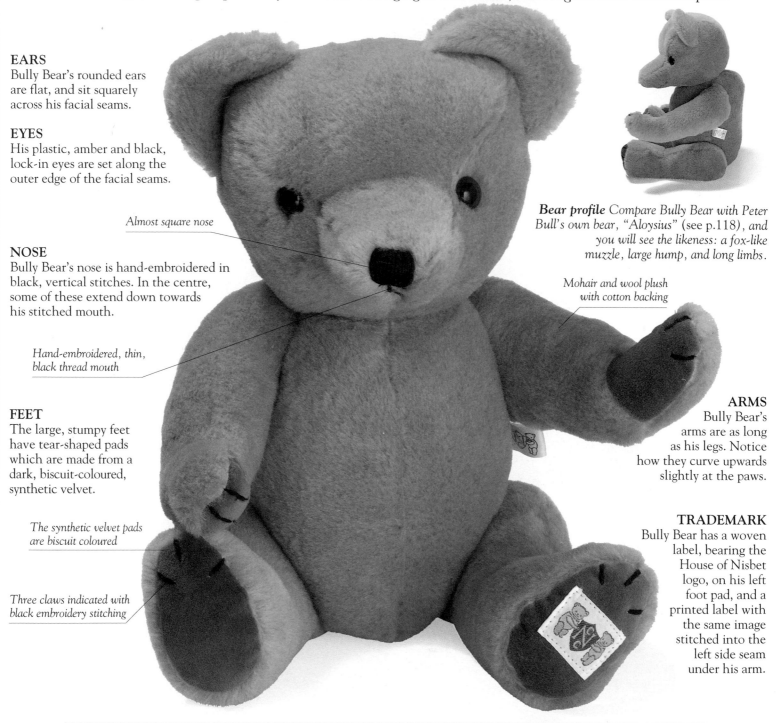

EARS
Bully Bear's rounded ears are flat, and sit squarely across his facial seams.

EYES
His plastic, amber and black, lock-in eyes are set along the outer edge of the facial seams.

Almost square nose

NOSE
Bully Bear's nose is hand-embroidered in black, vertical stitches. In the centre, some of these extend down towards his stitched mouth.

Hand-embroidered, thin, black thread mouth

FEET
The large, stumpy feet have tear-shaped pads which are made from a dark, biscuit-coloured, synthetic velvet.

The synthetic velvet pads are biscuit coloured

Three claws indicated with black embroidery stitching

Bear profile *Compare Bully Bear with Peter Bull's own bear, "Aloysius" (see p.118), and you will see the likeness: a fox-like muzzle, large hump, and long limbs.*

Mohair and wool plush with cotton backing

ARMS
Bully Bear's arms are as long as his legs. Notice how they curve upwards slightly at the paws.

TRADEMARK
Bully Bear has a woven label, bearing the House of Nisbet logo, on his left foot pad, and a printed label with the same image stitched into the left side seam under his arm.

• BEAR ESSENTIALS •

HT: 45cm (18in)

FUR: golden, mohair and wool plush
EYES: amber, safe, plastic, black pupils
EARS: medium, rounded, flat, sit squarely
MUZZLE: very long and pointed, fox-like

NOSE: hand-embroidered, squarish, black
ARMS: curved; synthetic pads; claws
FEET: large; synthetic pads; claws
STUFFING: synthetic wadding

Trademark

⇌ *Flash* ⇌

1980 CANTERBURY BEARS

Flash was the first bear manufactured by this family business, established in 1980. From their home in Canterbury, England, John and Maude Blackburn and their three children still produce a variety of traditional teddy bears as well as individual commissions for exporting around the world. (Replicas of Flash are available.)

EARS
Flash's peculiarly large and floppy ears hang from the sides of his head, in a similar manner to those of the 1930s "Miss Jessie Criddle" *(see p.60).*

Old-fashioned spectacles

ARMS
His relatively short, fat arms only taper slightly towards the paws.

Huge, plastic amber, safe, lock-in eyes

FUR
The fur is long, light brown man-made fabric with a knitted back. The plush on Flash's replica has a woven back.

FEET
Flash's large feet and narrow pads are similar to the ones found on early bears.

Cream, chamois leather pads

Bear profile *Seen from the side, Flash's extraordinarily long, floppy ears make him more reminiscent of a dog than a bear.*

Protruding, but blunt muzzle

NOSE
The moulded, plastic nose is more like the type used on 1950s bears, than the hand-embroidered detail of the early traditional models.

ACCESSORIES
Flash proudly wears a row of six British medals from the two World Wars, and an American medal given to him at a teddy bear show held in California. His spectacles enhance his distinguished appearance.

• BEAR ESSENTIALS •

FUR: light brown, long, artificial plush
EYES: large, amber, safe, plastic, black pupils
EARS: large, floppy, hang from sides of head
MUZZLE: large, blunt and protruding

NOSE: moulded plastic, realistic, black
ARMS: thick; cream, leather pads; no claws
FEET: large; cream, leather pads; no claws
STUFFING: synthetic

HT: 84cm (33in)

Trademark

❧ "*Johann*" ❧

HERMANN-SPIELWAREN, COBURG

"Johann" is one of thousands of fine quality, hand-made teddy bears exported by this successful German soft toy manufacturer. Hermann-Spielwaren GmbH is now based in Coburg, and run by Rolf Hermann, Max Hermann's son and Johann Hermann's grandson.

Bear profile *"Johann's" long, protruding muzzle, straight back, short arms, and small feet distinguish him from traditional teddy bears.*

EARS
"Johann" has particularly small, flat ears, which are positioned squarely over the seams of his face.

EYES
The amber and black glass eyes are attached to the bear's face with wire shanks. They are positioned on the outside of the facial seams, and the edge of the muzzle.

Clipped mohair plush on muzzle

TRADEMARK
The Hermann-Spielwaren metal tag is always attached to the bear's chest with a red cord.

Long mohair plush

FEET
His feet are very small, and his ankles are not well defined. The tear-shaped pads are made from flesh-coloured felt, and match those on his paws.

NOSE AND MOUTH
The thin, lozenge-shaped nose at the end of the muzzle consists of a few horizontal stitches in black thread. A vertical stitch extends from his nose to his inverted, V-shaped mouth.

Three distinctive black thread claws on both paws and feet

ARMS
The short, tapering arms have thick shoulders, and thin paws that curve slightly upwards.

• BEAR ESSENTIALS •

HT: 48cm (19in)

FUR: golden, mohair plush; some clipped
EYES: medium, amber, glass, black pupils
EARS: small, flat, squarely over face seams
MUZZLE: protuding, clipped mohair plush

NOSE: hand-embroidered, black
ARMS: short; flesh-coloured, felt pads; claws
FEET: small; flesh-coloured, felt pads; claws
STUFFING: wood-wool throughout bear

Trademark

❧ *Original Teddy* ❧

1990 STEIFF

Every few years, Steiff create a modern version of one of their original bears. Petsy, Molly, and Zotty have all been honoured in this way. New, Original Teddy bears, based on Steiff's 1905 bear, have been made in various colours and sizes, and have been one of their most popular lines for more than 20 years.

EARS
Set high on the head, the inner edges of the ears are caught in the face seams, so they turn outwards.

EYES
His eyes are made from brown and black plastic. As required by law for children's soft toys, they are the safe, lock-in variety.

Heart-shaped muzzle – a move away from the traditional style

VOICE BOX
This particular bear contains a tilt growler, although the same model is also available with a squeaker.

FUR
Long, honey-coloured mohair plush is used for the bear's body, head and limbs; only his muzzle is clipped.

FEET
Following Steiff tradition, Original Teddy has large feet, but the beige foot pads are made from Draylon.

Legs are shorter than those of the early Steiff bears

Bear profile *Like early bears, Original Teddy has a protruding muzzle, realistic feet, and curved, tapering arms. However, his hump has disappeared, his head is rounder, and his legs are shorter than his arms.*

Original red bow

NOSE AND MOUTH
The nose is hand-embroidered in brown thread. The mouth is in a similar coloured thread and adjoins the nose: there is no vertical stitch between the two.

Steiff tag secured to the chest

ARMS
His arms are tapered, and curve upwards at the paws like the arms of his ancestors.

TRADEMARK
Even nowadays, Steiff uses the *Knopf im Ohr* ("button in ear") trademark.

• BEAR ESSENTIALS •

HT: 36cm (14in)

FUR: honey-coloured, long, mohair plush
EYES: brown, safe, plastic, black pupils
EARS: small, outward-turning, high on head
MUZZLE: protruding, clipped mohair plush

NOSE: hand-embroidered, oval, brown
ARMS: long; beige, Draylon pads; no claws
FEET: large; beige, Draylon pads; no claws
STUFFING: synthetic

Made in Germany by Steiff
KNOPF IM OHR
0201/51
Trademark

❧ "Michael" ❧

1987 DEAN'S CO. (1903) LTD.

*An international take-over in 1986 gave Dean's Rag Book Co. Ltd. a new name: Dean's Co. Ltd..
In 1990, they revived their old name, however, and launched a new line in reproduction bears. The firm still
operates from Pontypool in Wales, where they have been based since 1974.*

EARS
"Michael" has small, flat ears. The inner edges of each ear are caught in the facial seams; the rest is placed on the side of his head.

Safe, lock-in eyes made from amber and black plastic

ACCESSORIES
"Michael" is sold with a smart red ribbon tied round his neck. He comes in a drawstring, printed, calico bag, instead of a box.

Stitched U-shaped mouth

London-gold wool and mohair plush

FEET
His feet are relatively long and wide. The narrow, oval pads are made of brown, synthetic velveteen.

Short, stumpy legs and big feet

Bear profile "Michael" has a rounded head and protruding muzzle. Notice his unusually square shoulders, his short legs, and arms with hooked paws.

Muzzle made from a separate piece of fabric to the head

NOSE
The nose is embroidered in black thread to form a triangular shape. No vertical stitch joins the nose with the mouth.

ARMS
The tapered arms are particularly short with narrow, almost hook-like, paws. The pads match those on his feet.

TRADEMARK
A woven, folded label, showing the company's new name, is sewn into the side seam under the left arm. A folded, printed card (not visible here) is sewn into his left ear.

❧ BEAR ESSENTIALS ❧

HT: 48cm (19in)

FUR: London gold, wool and mohair plush
EYES: amber, safe, plastic, black pupils
EARS: small, flat, placed wide apart
MUZZLE: protruding, separate fabric piece

NOSE: hand-embroidered, triangular, black
ARMS: short; brown, synthetic pads; no claws
FEET: wide; brown, synthetic pads; no claws
STUFFING: polyurethane foam granules

Trademark

☙ "Watty Watford" ☙

1982 R. DAKIN & CO.

"Watty Watford" a Woolie Bear was produced by R. Dakin & Co., San Francisco, as part of a range of bears. Founded in 1955, the firm originally imported toys, among other goods. It was not until the 1970s that they established themselves as soft toy manufacturers.

The muzzle occupies the entire face

EYES
His clear, plastic eyes, with brown backs and black pupils, are safely locked into the fabric with washers that pass through the face seams. Dakin is renowned for its high safety standards, so the eyes would have undergone rigorous stress tests, probably greater than those dictated by government safety regulations.

A very round, bulbous head

EARS
The small ears are wide and narrow. They are secured to the sides of his head.

Unjointed arms hang straight down the sides of the body

TRADEMARK
A folded, fabric label sewn into the back seam gives details of the materials used to make the bear. He also has a swing tag secured to his neck.

At the paw ends, the arms are slightly wider

FEET
When removed, his socks reveal wide, pear-shaped pads made from the same material as the rest of his body – white wool pile on a polyester backing.

Bear profile *"Watty Watford" has straight, unjointed arms and legs. His legs are sewn to the front of his body, so he is permanently in the sitting position.*
Hand-embroidered, brown, wool mouth

NOSE
Hand-embroidered vertical stitches in brown wool form a triangle at the point where the two face seams join at the muzzle.

FUR
"Watty Watford" is made from a white, plush material, consisting of a short, wool pile, on a polyester, machine-knitted backing. The Woolie Bear range was also available in a gold plush.

ACCESSORIES
"Watty Watford" wears a striped scarf and socks. The gold Woolie Bear wears the same outfit in green and beige wool. The smaller Wee Woolie Bear, wears only a scarf.

☙ "Knebbyworth" ❧

1985 NAOMI LAIGHT

"Knebbyworth" is the work of British teddy bear artist, Naomi Laight, who has made old-style collectors' bears from her home since the 1980s. The bear's present owner bought him during a "Save the Children" charity tour of bears, at Knebworth House, Hertfordshire, in England, hence his name.

EARS
"Knebbyworth's" small ears are folded almost completely in half, and the inner part is sewn into the facial seam. This makes them lie back flat and face outwards.

EYES
The large, flat, black plastic buttons resemble the flat, metal buttons used in the early British bear (*see p.30*). These, however, have plastic loops sewn into the face with strong cotton.

NOSE AND MOUTH
Black wool, vertical stitches respresent his oval nose. A few stitches in the centre extend down to the inverted, V-shaped mouth.

CLAWS
Both the feet and the paws have four black wool claws, sewn onto the mohair plush.

Long, thin muzzle

Bear profile "Knebbyworth" resembles the bears made before World War I. He has a long, pointed nose, small, laid-back ears, a slight hump on his back, long limbs and curved paws.

TRADEMARK
"Knebbyworth" has a woven, cream label sewn onto his back with the words, "A Naomi Laight Collectors' Bear" embroidered in silk.

Long, tapering arms, curved at the paws

Short pile mohair plush

Large, narrow feet

Brown suede pads

• BEAR ESSENTIALS •

HT: 33cm (13in)

FUR: dark khaki, short pile, mohair plush
EYES: large, flat, black, plastic buttons
EARS: small, folded, lie flat at back of head
MUZZLE: long, thin, extends from forehead

NOSE: hand-embroidered, oval, black
ARMS: long; brown, suede pads; claws
FEET: large; brown, suede pads; claws
STUFFING: grey/beige cotton flock

Trademark

A Naomi Laight
COLLECTORS BEAR

❧ "Woody Herman" ❧

1985 APPLAUSE (DESIGNED BY ROBERT RAIKES)

Robert Raikes produces unique teddy bears and other animals, with individually carved wooden faces and feet, from his studio in northern California. Applause, who markets his work, was once a division of the Knickerbocker Toy Co. who merged with Wallace Berrie and Co. in 1984. Applause market this bear as Jamie.

EYES

The small, clear plastic eyes are glued into recesses carved into his wooden face. The pupils are suggested with holes drilled into the wood behind his eyes.

Small flat ears sewn into a seam running around the head

FUR AND STUFFING

The knitted synthetic plush covering "Woody Herman" is a mixture of light brown and black fibres, giving him a tabby-like appearance. He is stuffed with a soft, synthetic wadding.

Short, tapered arms, notable for their lack of paw pads and claws

FEET

The feet are not very well-defined. The oval, rounded pads are made of smooth wood, lacquered to a golden sheen.

Bear profile *"Woody Herman's" large, rounded head, and protruding, carved, wooden muzzle, are offset by a touch of realism – a stubby tail, an unusual feature on a teddy bear.*

Carefully chiselled mouth gives the bear a winsome expression

MUZZLE

The muzzle and nose are all part of a carved, wooden mask, stained golden brown. The shiny, button-like nose is carved out of the same piece of wood, and stained black.

ACCESSORIES

A small booklet giving washing instructions, safety standards, and background information on the subject of the designer, Robert Raikes, is sold with this bear.

• BEAR ESSENTIALS •

HT: 23cm (9in)

FUR: brown and black mix, synthetic plush
EYES: small, clear, plastic, glued to wood mask
EARS: small, flat, placed wide apart
MUZZLE: carved wood, stained brown

NOSE: carved wood, round, stained black
ARMS: short, tapered; no pads or claws
FEET: small; brown, wooden pads; no claws
STUFFING: synthetic wadding

Trademark

❧ Brian's Bear ❧

c.1987 ASQUITHS

Brian's Bear was designed by teddy bear artist and repairer, Brian Beacock, for Joan Bland of Asquiths, the first shop in Britain exclusively selling teddy bears. Asquiths opened in Windsor in 1984, and two more shops followed in Henley-on-Thames and Eton. Brian's Bear is a caricature of the traditional teddy bear.

EYES
The black plastic eyes are safely locked into the fabric with washers. At a glance, they resemble the boot buttons used on early bears.

NOSE
His hand-embroidered nose consists of black wool, vertical stitches with horizontal stitches along the top.

Original red printed cravat – a blue paisley cravat is also available

VOICE BOX
A tilt growler in a plastic canister uses sliding bellows and a reed mechanism *(see p.93).*

FEET
The long, narrow feet are rounder and larger at their toe ends, a feature that is accentuated by the thin ankles.

Large, rounded ears are slighlty gathered

Bear profile The accentuated features caricaturing traditional teddy bear design are obvious: long limbs, curved paws, large feet, a long, pointed muzzle, and a humped back.

FUR
Brian's Bear is made from alpaca plush, a popular fabric for soft toys in Britain during the 1920s and 1930s. (Alpaca is llama fleece exported from Peru.)

Three black wool claws on each paw and each foot

Tear-shaped pads made from beige, synthetic fabric

STUFFING
Brian's Bear is stuffed throughout with kapok.

• BEAR ESSENTIALS •

HT: 40cm (16in)

FUR: fawn-coloured, natural alpaca plush
EYES: small, black, safe, plastic, lock-in
EARS: large, rounded, placed high on head
MUZZLE: long, thin, pointed, tapering

NOSE: hand-embroidered, black
ARMS: long; beige, synthetic pads; claws
FEET: long; beige, synthetic pads; claws
STUFFING: synthetic

DISTINGUISHING FEATURES: The smooth alpaca fur is an unusual feature on this bear. His caricatured design and the printed cravat are very distinctive.

❧ Sir Mortimer ❧

1990 NONSUCH SOFT TOYS

Named after the eminent British archaeologist, Sir Mortimer Wheeler, this limited edition bear was created by Susan Rixon to celebrate the 100th anniversary of the excavation of Silchester, a Roman town close to her home in Berkshire, England. Susan and her husband David have been making traditional bears since 1979.

EARS
Sir Mortimer's large and rounded ears are set centrally across the facial seams.

Eyes set wide apart

EYES
Like all of Susan's teddy bears, Sir Mortimer is fitted with safe, lock-in eyes. They are made of brown plastic.

VOICE BOX
Sir Mortimer contains a tilt growler even though he is not specifically intended for children. Many collectors' bears were made with voice boxes.

Long, spoon-shaped pads of orange velvet-like material

FEET
His feet are large and narrow in the traditional style, with long, oval pads of unusual, orange synthetic, velvet type fabric.

Bear profile The elongated muzzle, curved arms, and large feet are based on the traditional teddy bear style, but his slightly arched back reveals no hump.

Long, pointed muzzle

NOSE AND MOUTH
Black thread is used for Sir Mortimer's densely stitched nose and mouth.

Original printed bow tie

ARMS
His arms are long, curved, and tapered in the traditional manner. He has especially wide and high set shoulders.

TRADEMARK
A folded label is set into the back seam. All limited editions have authenticity certificates.

Dark brown, beige, and black mix mohair plush

❧ BEAR ESSENTIALS ❧

HT: 46cm (18in)

FUR: dark brown/beige/black mohair plush
EYES: brown, safe, plastic, black pupils
EARS: large, rounded, over face seams
MUZZLE: very long and pointed

NOSE: hand-embroidered, round, black
ARMS: long; orange, synthetic pads; no claws
FEET: large; orange, synthetic pads; no claws
STUFFING: synthetic

Nonsuch Mortimer Bear ©
Limited Edition of 200 only

Trademark

❧ *Freddie* ❧

1989 SUE E. FOSKEY

Freddie is one of 400 bears in a limited edition series, made by Sue E. Foskey, a teddy bear artist working from her home in Delaware, New Jersey. Sue has been designing delightful teddies since 1984; her most recent work includes "antique-look" bears, made from distressed mohair, and dressed in period clothing.

EARS
Large, flat ears sit on the sides of his head. They resemble the ears of Steiff bears made at the beginning of the century.

Thin, pointed muzzle

EYES
Freddie was made for the collectors' market, so he did not have to meet the safety standards required for children's toys. He could, therefore, have glass bead eyes on wire stalks, similar to those used on small bears in the early years of teddy bear production.

TRADEMARK
Sue Foskey's signature, together with the number of the edition (46/400, showing that he was the 46th bear out of 400 produced) is written on the bear's right foot. His left foot carries a printed label bearing the designer's name and the date of manufacture.

Claws stitched across the plush

FEET
Freddie has large feet, with long, narrow, oval pads of beige felt. The four claws are shown with black thread.

Designer's signature and limited edition number

Bear profile *Freddie's pointed muzzle, thin body, long and tapering arms and legs, and large feet, are all features borrowed from earlier bears.*

Black thread mouth

NOSE
His rectangular nose is made up from horizontal stitches of black thread. They are sewn across the tip of his muzzle.

A chic, lilac bow, and a tiny cluster of flowers, add to Freddie's charms

ARMS
The long, tapering arms are relatively wide at the shoulders. The paws are both narrow and curved.

FUR
Freddie is made from brown, mohair plush. However, the muzzle is clipped, and reveals the woven backing.

• BEAR ESSENTIALS •

HT: 25cm (10in)

FUR: light brown, mohair plush
EYES: small, black, glass beads
EARS: large, flat, set on sides of head
MUZZLE: thin, pointed, clipped

NOSE: hand-embroidered, rectangular, black
ARMS: long; beige, felt pads; claws
FEET: large; beige, felt pads; claws
STUFFING: kapok throughout bear

FREDDIE
© 1989 Sue Foskey

Trademark

❧ The Bride ❧

1990 DEE HOCKENBERRY

The Bride was made for the collectors' market. She is a typical, sugar-sweet creation of well-established teddy bear artist, Dee Hockenberry, who is based in Albion, New York State. A dealer in collectable Steiff animals and teddy bears, Dee is also a well-known writer of books and articles on the subject.

EARS
The Bride's large, flat ears are set wide apart, leaving plenty of room for her elaborate lace and bead head-dress.

Protruding muzzle

EYES
Unlike the majority of teddy bears made during this period, The Bride has glass eyes held on wire shanks, reverting to the old style. To comply with safety standards, she carries a warning which reads, "Not for Children under Four".

ACCESSORIES
The Bride's outfit consists of a short, lacy bolero and a head-dress of the same material. Both are adorned with artificial flowers and sprays of white, plastic, pearl-like beads.

Four claws extend across the plush and felt pads

White felt pads match the colour of the mohair plush

Folded, printed label, sewn into left leg seam

Bear profile *The Bride has a pert, upturned, muzzle, and large feet reminiscent of the early Steiff bears. Her arms, which bend at the elbow, are a break from tradition.*

Amber glass eyes with black pupils

NOSE AND MOUTH
The triangular nose, and the mouth, are hand-stitched with pinkish-brown embroidery thread. The nose is similar both in style and colour to the 1921 white Steiff bear (see p.42).

ARMS
The Bride has unusual arms which bend at the elbows. They are a little like Steiff's Teddy Baby of 1930 (see p.49).

• BEAR ESSENTIALS •

HT: 33cm (13in)

FUR: white, mohair plush
EYES: medium, amber, glass, black pupils
EARS: large, flat, positioned wide apart
MUZZLE: pert, protruding and upturned

NOSE: hand-stitched, triangular, pink-brown
ARMS: long, bent; white, felt pads; claws
FEET: large, narrow; white, felt pads; claws
STUFFING: kapok throughout bear

TRADEMARK: The Bride had a folded, printed label, carrying the artist's name. It was stitched into the seam at the back of her left leg.

❧ THE MODERN BEAR ❧

In recent years teddy bear collecting, or arctophily, has become an internationally recognized hobby. The growing interest in teddy bears has caused saleroom prices to escalate; in 1989, a Steiff bear was auctioned at Sotheby's for an extraordinary £55,000 ($86,000). Increased demand has led to several cases of fraud, with Steiff or Bing buttons being attached to bears in an attempt to increase value. Today, experts study the history of the teddy bear; collectors' magazines are published in the United States, Great Britain, and Australia; and Teddy Bear Conventions are held, particularly in the United States, where events are staged annually in Baltimore, Orlando, Toledo, and San Diego.

A SERIOUS BUSINESS

Teddy bears have become serious business and several museums dedicated to them now exist. Among the best known are, Florentine Wagner's collection in Berlin; Colin Wilson's in Queensland, Australia; and in England, Gyles Brandreth's in Stratford-upon-Avon. One of the most recent additions is Franny's Teddy Bear Museum in Florida, which opened in 1990. Several of the major soft toy manufacturers now display some of their early samples and they have also published their histories. Steiff has a museum located within their factory complex in Giengen. Merrythought, too, has documented its history, and several of their factory samples feature at their small museum in the town of Ironbridge, Shropshire, England.

△ **Museum Piece**
A curator at the Bethnal Green Museum of Childhood, in London, catalogues a new acquisition before putting it on display.

△ **1930s Replica**
Made by Canterbury Bears, Theodore, is a modern bear, based on a 1930s design.

TEDDY BEAR RESTORATION

The number of expert restorers has risen in response to the growing demand for repairs to tattered teds saved from the backs of cupboards and garages. As early as 1972, an amusing survey was written by veterinary surgeons, Blackmore and Young, entitled "Some Observations of the Diseases of *Brunus Edwardii*". This highly scientific paper discussed, among other problems, cases of soggy ear, ruptured frontal seam, and alopecia (hair loss). To deal with these afflictions, special products have been developed in the United States for bear care. Teddy bear dust covers, and a cleaning fluid made by the Bear Care Co., are two examples.

TRADITIONAL BEARS

Large manufacturers, such as Steiff, Hermann, Gund, Merrythought, and Deans, are responding to the passion for old teds by producing traditional humped-backed, long limbed and muzzled designs, often in limited editions. Other examples of the attempt to capture past moments

△ **Teddy Auctions**
Auction houses, Sotheby's, Christie's, and Phillips, all have sales devoted to teddy bears and other toys. They will undertake valuations, unlike the museums.

▷ **Collectors' Paradise**
Judy Sparrow has an extensive collection on show at her Teddy Bear museum in Petersfield, Hampshire, England. She also sells modern collectors' bears and runs a repair service for old teddies.

in the teddy bear's history include the delightful Steiff Berryman Bear, based on the cartoonist Berryman's original, *Washington Post* illustration and designed by Linda Mullins. The House of Nisbet revived the Schuco-invented Yes/No bears in 1988 and Bedford Bears recently introduced a range of blue bears similar to those popular between the 1930s and 1950s. Steiff pioneered the concept of reproducing bears from their archives for the collectors' market. Replicas are also being made of bears with interesting backgrounds, such as the Steiff, "Alfonzo" (*see p.118*) and "Happy" (*see p.45*), "Delicatessen" (*see p.119*), and "Gatti", the little 1907 Bing bear, who survived the sinking of the Titanic in 1912.

ANNIVERSARY BEARS

Many older companies are also producing limited edition bears to mark special anniversaries. In 1978 Ideal made a birthday bear to celebrate their 75th anniversary; Hermann did the same to mark their 75th birthday in 1982; Gund celebrated their 85th birthday in 1983, and Merrythought announced 60 years of age in 1990 (*see p.120*). The more recent companies have followed suit: British firms, Canterbury Bears (*see p.121*), and Bedford Bears, made special bears on their tenth anniversaries in 1990. Some museums have commissioned companies to manufacture special bears for them.

△ **Toy Store Bear**
The Hamley's Bear was specially made by Steiff for Hamley's toy store in London.

REPLICA BEARS

The teddy bear collecting boom of the 1980s, and the accompanying price rise of antique teddy bears in the salerooms, inspired some of the old manufacturers to produce replicas of their older lines. Their intention was to provide collectors with old-looking bears at more reasonable prices. Ironically many of these replicas are now increasing in value and some are extremely expensive. Steiff, Hermann, and Dean have all produced replicas.

1905 RICHARD STEIFF TEDDY REPLICA
First reproduced in 1980, this little grey bear represents the prototype teddy bear that Richard Steiff first developed in 1905. His blunt nose and wide ears were distinguishing features of all bears made at this factory until 1951. Richard Steiff's original bear was placed in the Steiff archives in the 1940s by his mother-in-law. He was one of two grey bears, perhaps made as samples. He is particularly special because his foot was signed in 1983 by Hans Otto Steiff, the great-great nephew of Margarete Steiff, the inspiration behind the Steiff firm.

1909 TEDDY BEAR REPLICA
Replicas of the 1909 teddy bear were first made, in two sizes, in 1984. They were so popular that three more sizes were made. Like its original model, the replica is made of woven mohair plush. Its stuffing is not wood-wool, but synthetic fibre. To conform with modern safety standards, its eyes, which in 1909 would have been sewn-in boot buttons, are made of moulded plastic, secured into the fabric with a washer. In one ear, there is a yellow and red woven tag with a button sewn in.

Steiff's trademark

Moulded plastic eyes

Otto Steiff's signature

TEDDY ROSE REPLICA

This shaggy, pink, mohair plush teddy, first reproduced in 1988, is a replica of Teddy Rose, one of an unusual line of 5,000 bears made by Steiff from 1925-1930. Unlike the previous two replicas described, Teddy Rose, was made as a limited edition of 10,000 world-wide, a point noted on the bear's printed, card, chest label. The number (0170) refers to the product. This is followed by the bear's height in centimetres (41). The reverse of the label carries the number of this particular edition; this is reproduced on the guarantee of authenticity certificate that accompanies the bear in a special presentation box. A smaller Teddy Rose, 25cm (10in) in height, was made in a limited edition of 8,000 in 1990. Like the larger replica, he has compact, wood-wool stuffing that makes him heavy.

STEIFF
Teddy Rose
Replica 1925
Ltd. Ed. 10 000
1987-1988

Δ **Card Chest Labels**
A modernized card chest label, similar to those used on 1928-1950 bears.

STEIFF SNAP-APART-BEAR REPLICA 1908

First reproduced in 1990, this unusual bear is a replica of an original factory sample for the 1908 Druckknopf (snap fastener) Bär 5353, who was never sold to the public. Snap fasteners had been invented by the German, Carl August Pfenning, in 1895. Their intended use was to button the flies on men's trousers! Steiff borrowed the new invention to produce a series of seven soft toys for young children. These toys consisted of a round body with head and limbs attached by snap fasteners. When the head and limbs are removed, the toy becomes a rather unusual throw ball. This little white bear is only 18cm (7in) high when complete. When he is pulled apart, you can see Carl Pfenning's patent number clearly impressed around each snap fastener. Along with a golliwog, this bear was one of Steiff's early experiments. In 1909, this ingenious design was patented as one of Steiff's Roly Poly Toys.

Steiff's button-in-ear trademark

Snap-off arms

"ALFONZO": FRIEND OF A RUSSIAN PRINCESS

In 1908, George Mikhailovich, the Grand Duke of Russia, commissioned Steiff to make this bear for his daughter, Princess Xenia Georgievna. His owner took him to England in 1914, where they were guests of the Russian princess's royal relatives at Buckingham Palace. The outbreak of World War I prevented the princess and her bear from returning home, an event that saved Princess Xenia from certain death in the Russian Revolution. "Alfonzo" became a treasured possession as he was the only gift that she had brought from her homeland, given to her by the father she adored. "Alfonzo's" rarity, and his unusual background, accounted for the fact that he was sold at a Christie's auction in May 1989 for £12,100 ($19,800), then a world record. From the London salerooms, he travelled to his new home in the Cotswold village of Witney, near Oxford, England, where he is presently on permanent display at his owner's antique and collectors' teddy bear shop. "Alfonzo" is a unique Steiff bear made of a short rust-red mohair plush, with beige, felt paws. His nose is slightly worn and the holes in his paws reveal his traditional wood-wool stuffing.

1990 "ALFONZO": REPLICA

Following the purchase of the unique "Alfonzo", the new owners made an arrangement with the present Steiff company to produce a replica bear that they could sell exclusively in their shop, where a number of other collector bears were already available. The replica "Alfonzo" was first produced in a limited edition of 5,000 in 1990. See how faithfully he follows the original: he is the same height (33cm/13in); he wears an identical white-trimmed, orange cotton sateen suit, with trousers held up by braces, beneath a contemporary Russian-style tunic with a side fastening. Although he is not as worn as the real "Alfonzo", his unusual red plush has a light brown woven backing. The "Alfonzo" replica is packed in a smart dark green presentation box, with his history and the edition number printed on a special certificate of authenticity. The large, brass-coloured metal button, with incised cursive script, and the white printed collectors' tag in the ear, indicate that he is a replica. The original "Alfonzo" has the smaller nickel 1905-1950 button with raised capital letters.

Rust-red mohair plush

Worn felt pad

Russian-style tunic

Steiff's button-in-ear trademark

"ALOYSIUS": BRIDESHEAD HERO

Like "Alphonzo", "Delicatessen" is a much-travelled bear. He began life in about 1907, possibly in the New York-based, Ideal Toy Co. factory. In 1969, he was given to the late British actor and arctophile, Peter Bull, following his television appearance on the American *Johnny Carson Show*. Peter Bull christened him "Delicatessen". A little over a decade later, however, the bear officially changed his name, by deed poll, to "Aloysius", following his acting debut as Sebastian's teddy bear in the British television series based on Evelyn Waugh's *Brideshead Revisited*. Filming took him to Venice, and the United States. When Peter Bull died in 1984, "Aloysius" was bequeathed to the actor's friend, Don Busby, and later displayed in the Teddy Bear Museum in Stratford-upon-Avon, England. This world-famous octogenarian returned to his homeland in 1989 to reside with his present owners, American teddy collectors, Rosemary and Paul Volpp.

▽ *"Brideshead" Star*
"Aloysius" in the television series
Brideshead Revisited.

1987 "ALOYSIUS": REPLICA

Many of "Delicatessen's" features had already been copied by the House of Nisbet, in their Bully Bear (*see p.102*), but it was not until his television success that a replica was made in 1987. The distressed mohair plush, seen on the replica, below, is used by several contemporary makers of traditional teddy bears. It was invented by Nisbet's Jack Wilson, in conjunction with Norton (Weaving) Ltd. of Yorkshire, using a 1904 velvet-crushing machine. The chamois leather patches on the limbs and body of the replica bear are identical to those on the original; indeed the likeness, in general, is so close that it is really only the House of Nisbet woven label that gives away the replica bear's identity. Each replica comes with a copy of the Daks Simpson scarf, presented to the bear by his co-star, Anthony Andrews' wife, and a British Airways flight bag, denoting his well-travelled career. Originally the replicas were to be called "Aloysius" but the North American Bear Co. had already bought the copyright for reproducing the bear, and so the replica used the bear's initial name, "Delicatessen".

Distressed mohair plush

ANNIVERSARY BEARS

This special limited edition bear was produced to mark the 60th birthday of Merrythought Ltd., one of the oldest surviving, British, soft toy manufacturers. Similar in style to the 1930s designs, the Diamond Jubilee Bear was launched in June 1990, at the famous London store of Harrods. He comes in a royal blue presentation box. He has a limited edition tag signed by the managing director, grandson of the firm's founder, stitched into his left seam.

EARS
Diamond Jubilee has large, flat, rounded ears, set on the side of his head. They are similar to those on Chummy (*see p.53*), one of his older relatives.

EYES
His brown and black plastic eyes are the safe, lock-in type. They are positioned on the outer edge of the facial seams, and next to the muzzle.

Original bow

VOICE BOX
A modern tilt growler is fitted into his body.

Pale, golden mohair with feather finish

ARMS
The shoulders are high, and the bear's long, tapering arms end in curved paws.

Beige, Draylon pads on large feet

Bear profile *The pointed, clipped muzzle, large ears, hint of a hump on the back, and long, curved limbs, make this bear similar to the early Merrythought designs.*

NOSE
The triangular nose consists of black thread vertical stitches.

Three claws stitched across mohair

Limited edition tag

TRADEMARK
The trademark is set on a Union Jack, sewn to the right foot pad.

• BEAR ESSENTIALS •

HT: 45cm (18in)

FUR: pale gold, mohair plush, some clipped
EYES: amber, safe, plastic, black pupils
EARS: large, flat, rounded, on sides of head
MUZZLE: protruding, pointed, clipped

NOSE: hand-embroidered, triangular, black
ARMS: long, tapering; beige, Draylon pads; claws
FEET: large; beige, Draylon pads; claws
STUFFING: wood-wool; polyester

Trademark

PRIVATE ISSUE NOT FOR RESALE 35/40 Oliver Holmel

Launched in April 1990, this large bear celebrates the 10th anniversary of a family business, based just outside the ancient cathedral city of Canterbury, in Kent, England. The firm produces 50,000 bears a year, but the anniversary bear is one of a limited edition of just 500. The 10th Anniversary Bear follows the traditional teddy bear design; he has long limbs, a humped back, and a pointed nose.

Close-set eyes

Thin, black wool mouth

EARS
The small, rounded ears are placed in the corners of his large, squarish head. The inside of the ear is made from the same suede fabric that is used for the foot and paw pads.

EYES
His amber and black, plastic, lock-in eyes are set low down on his face, giving him a high forehead.

Original bow

FEET
The feet are large. Maude and John Blackburn, who own Canterbury Bears, have signed the suede pad on his right foot.

CLAWS
Each black wool claw is indicated with two stitches: one stitch reaches across the suede pad; the other stretches across the mohair plush.

Three black wool claws on each paw

Large suede pads

Bear profile *Like so many modern collector's bears, he is a caricature of traditional teddy design, with his humped back, long limbs, and protruding, pointed muzzle.*

NOSE
The nose is hand-embroidered. Vertical stitches of black wool create a slightly wider nose than those found on other bears manufactured by this firm.

ARMS
His arms are exceptionally long, and they are placed very high on his body. They taper and curve into long, beige, suede-padded paws.

TRADEMARK
A woven label featuring Canterbury City's Coat of Arms, an honour bestowed on the firm in 1987, is sewn into the left side seam.

Five claws on each foot

• BEAR ESSENTIALS •

HT: 66cm (26in)

FUR: biscuit coloured, mohair plush
EYES: small, amber, safe, plastic, black pupils
EARS: small, rounded, suede inner ear
MUZZLE: protruding, pointed

NOSE: hand-embroidered, rectangular, black
ARMS: long, tapering, large suede pads; claws
FEET: large; oval suede pads; claws
STUFFING: polyester

THE WORKING BEAR

Teddy Roosevelt's bear began life as a mascot, and the tradition continues today, with teddy bears lending their support to political, sporting, and charitable causes. Rupert Bear, for example, is used to promote a charity that helps people suffering from muscular dystrophy, and Paddington Bear has a club that contributes to the British charity, "Action Research for the Crippled Child". There is no doubt that, over the years, the teddy bear has assumed an important role as a universal comforter and a symbol of friendship and security.

GOOD BEARS OF THE WORLD

Many unique teddy bears have been produced in recent times to help children with special needs. There are bears designed to help fretful babies sleep: The Kamar Toy Co.'s Dear Heart bear has a battery operated heart that beats like a human mother's. There is also a bear made to help the profoundly deaf, whose red eyes light up on hearing words. In Britain, Bill Bear was designed for chemical-sensitive children by Mary Holden, a fellow sufferer. Teddy bears have also proved a powerful support in distressing situations. In one French hospital, for example, prior to surgery, children are guided through an operation, using their teddy bears as patients, to help disband fear. In the United States, the Colorado police use the Celestial Seasonings Tea Co.'s Sleepy Time Bear to help young victims of accident and abuse.

The teddy bear's role as soulmate and confessor, led to the founding of "Good Bears of the World", an international fund-raising organization, providing

△ **Olympic Mascot**
The 1980 Olympic Games used Mishka, a bear from Russian folklore, as its mascot.

△ **Bear for the Disabled**
Made in the United States, these bears are designed to help disabled children come to terms with their handicap.

◁ **Tom Foolery**
A limited edition of 150 "Tom Foolery" bears made for Walt Disney World's Second Annual Teddy Bear Convention in Florida, in 1989. The bears were made by Doris and Terry Michaud.

teddy bears for both hospitalised children and adults, as well as the old and frail, in nursing homes, or children in care. The brainchild of American journalist, James T. Ownby, it was inaugurated in Berne, Switzerland, in 1973. Until Ownby's death in 1986, the organization was based at his home in Honolulu, Hawaii, but it now operates from Ohio, United States. There are over 10,000 world-wide members, organized into groups – "dens" who buy and distribute teddy bears to worthy causes.

FUND RAISING

In the United States, the official Good Bears of the World Bear was made by Ideal in the 1980s, and now by Dakin. Theodore Roosevelt's birthday, 27 October, has been designated Good Bear Day, and so fund-raising events involving teddies often occur then. In Britain, however, the first great teddy bear rally was on 27 May 1979, when 15,000 people and 2,000 teddy bears met in the grounds of Longleat, the Wiltshire home of the Marquis of Bath and his teddy bear, "Clarence". It initiated more rallies in Britain, as well as New Zealand, and Australia. In the United States, the teddy bear conventions, where enthusiasts meet to exchange ideas, stories, and bears, are particularly popular. Teddy bears are also used for fund raising. In Britain, for example, the sale of a white bear called "William" raises money for the Royal Marsden, the country's foremost cancer hospital, and Merrythought's replica of a teddy bear owned by British actress, Dame Judi Dench, raises money for the charity, "The Child Psychotherapy Trust".

△ **Police Help**
Teddy bears, often donated by "Good Bears of the World", working with American police to help traumatised children.

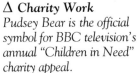

△ **Charity Work**
Pudsey Bear is the official symbol for BBC television's annual "Children in Need" charity appeal.

▷ **From Sri Lanka with Love**
This candlewick teddy bear is a gift from the people of Sri Lanka to "Good Bears of the World".

△ **The Marquis of Bath**
Residents of Longleat.

△ **Teddy Bear's Picnic**
Bears belonging to the late Colonel Bob Henderson, founder member of the UK branch of "Good Bears of the World", and a leading light in arctophily.

CARE AND REPAIR

A teddy bear suffers from too much loving – he may lose an eye or an ear, his joints may weaken from being constantly held by one limb, or his stuffing might sag from being slept on for so many years. Minor operations may be performed at home, although it is always best to seek advice. Bears can be lightly sponged with a diluted, mild detergent, or brushed to remove surface dust, but they should never be completely submerged. Fortunately the number of expert restorers has increased over the last few years to meet the growing demand of war-torn teds. Detached limbs, unthreading noses, and dumb growlers can all be resurrected, with care and patience.

EVERYDAY BEAR CARE

It is worth remembering that a teddy is a textile, and he is therefore affected by light, dust, damp, and the combined traumas of every-day life – insects, vermin, bacteria, and most common of all, over-affectionate children and dogs. Although the fibres of the materials will weaken and discolour with time, the following tips should prevent any further major damage. Keep a bear away from direct sunlight; make him clothes or change his position occasionally; gently vacuum or dust him regularly. Store him in a dry atmosphere, at a constant temperature, as warm, damp conditions encourage mould. Check him for insect life, such as the larvae of the carpet beetle, which leave a cobweb-like trail and oval casings. If any are found, seal the teddy in a polythene bag, with moth balls.

EYES
Lock-in eyes make the best replacements for a child's toy. Historical accuracy, however, dictates the more appropriate glass eyes. The wire shank is sewn in position, and a long needle takes the strong thread through to the back of the head, to be fastened off.

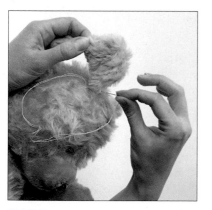

EARS
Ears are regularly torn or lost. This bear has a new ear, made from a similar plush. It is oversewn into place, ensuring that its position matches the other ear.

NOSE AND MOUTH
Thick embroidery silk is ideal for nose repair, although wool can be used, if care is taken to match the replacement thread with any original stitches.

GROWLER
Tilt growlers are removed through the bear's back seam. A new one may need padding out with extra stuffing.

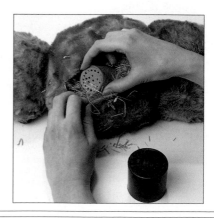

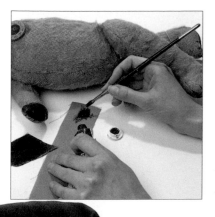

PAINTED PADS
English bears made between about 1930 and the late 1950s often had Rexine pads, an oilcloth that is no longer available. A similar fabric can be recreated by painting a muslin-type material with a quick-drying, brown paint. It can be cut to size and sewn in place.

ALL STITCHED UP
If a bear loses an arm or leg, a new one can be made from a similar piece of plush, matching the design to the remaining limb. Here a section of plush is machine-stitched on the wrong side, leaving a gap at the shoulder end, so that the stuffing and joints can be inserted.

PATCHING UP
The plush often wears thin at points where the bear has been regularly cuddled, or moth holes may develop over a period of time. Patching is best done beneath the hole, rather than over the top, either neatly oversewing into place or with invisible stitching.

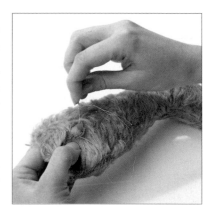

JOINTS
A cardboard disc and washer with a cotter pin inserted through the centre is being replaced. The pin will be pushed through the lower part of the body with the corresponding washer and disc behind it.

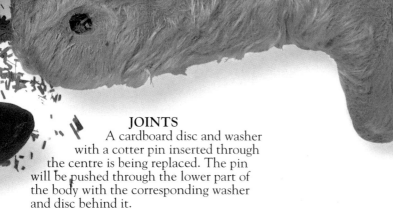

STUFFING
Teddies often have the stuffing quite literally knocked out of them. Wood-wool is ground to powder, or the kapok loses its youthful plumpness. The new stuffing can be replaced through one of the final handsewn seams.

FELT PADS
Felt pads can suffer from moths – or simply come adrift at the seams. The felt has been removed from this bear, and the new matching felt has been cut to size, and neatly oversewn into place.

INDEX

ACKNOWLEDGMENTS

Dorling Kindersley would like to thank the following, who generously lent their bears and associated memorabilia for special photography:
Timothy Atkinson 74; Brian Beacock 14, 15, 36, 37, 72, 73, 92, 93; Bear Essentials 97; Bethnal Green Museum of Childhood (a branch of the Victoria and Albert Museum) 5, 11, 13, 16, 17, 38, 39, 41, 47, 59, 82, 89, 98, 99, 100, 101, 102, 104, 106, 114; Heather Bischoff 28, 31; Gyles Brandreth, Teddy Bear Museum, Stratford-upon-Avon half-title page, title page, 6, 10, 11, 16, 18, 22, 23, 24, 38, 46, 69, 75, 76, 77, 78, 81, 94, 95, 96, 97, 111, 122, 123; Canterbury Bears 11, 103, 114; Pauline Cockrill 8, 9, 11, 67, 71, 72, 73, 79, 92, 93; Faith Eaton 11, 44; Nancy Evans 8, 11, 88; Lucinda Ganderton 8, 74, 75; Paul Goble 11, 49; Pam Hebbs title page, 5, 8, 9, 10, 11, 13, 16, 17, 18, 19, 21, 32, 34, 35, 38, 40, 42, 63, 71, 75, 77, 96, 97, 112, 113, 116, 117, 122; Peter Hebbs 97; Gillian Lister 66; London Toy and Model Museum 12, 86, 87; Merrythought Ltd. 120; Sheryl Nairn 50, 51; Ian Pout, "Teddy Bears" 5, 10, 11, 19, 33, 39, 40, 41, 64, 70, 118; Private Collection 5, 9, 10, 11, 17, 38, 60, 61, 62, 77, 85, 94, 95, 96, 107, 108, 109, 117, 119; David Robinson 8, 75; John Smith, The Doll's Hospital, Fulham, London 14, 15, 36, 37, 72, 73, 92, 93; Judy Sparrow, The Bear Museum, Petersfield 7, 10, 11, 18, 19, 30, 34, 35, 40, 41, 43, 48, 52, 53, 54, 55, 58, 71, 76, 83, 105, 114, 115, 124, 125; Paul and Rosemary Volpp 5, 11, 13, 20, 25, 26, 27, 29, 45, 65, 68, 69, 80, 119; Lynnet Wilson 8, 11, 84.

Thanks also to the following whose bears are currently on loan to the Teddy Bear Museum, Stratford-upon-Avon: Mike Reid (Sooty glove puppet) 76; Michael Bond (Paddington and bed) 86; Barbara Cartland (the Prince of Love) 90.

We are indebted to Irene Lyford, Damien Moore and Helen Townsend for their invaluable editorial help, and Marcus Hardy and Gillian Prince for additional editorial assistance; to Joanna Pocock for her design expertise; to Kate Grant and Susan Thompson for preliminary research; and to Emma Matthews for keying-in the text.

The author would like to thank the following people for all their help and advice:
Jacki Brooks of the Australian Doll Digest; Sylvia Coote; Glenn Jackman; Pat Rush; Pam Howells; John Blackburn of Canterbury Bears; Oliver Holmes of Merrythought Ltd.; Michael Crane of Dean's (1903) Company; Diane Phillips of Collins; Bunny Campione of Sotheby's; Judy and John Sparrow; Pam and Peter Hebbs; Brenda and Frank Faris; staff of the Bethnal Green Museum of Childhood; Sheryl and Mrs Nairn; John Smith of the Fulham Doll's Hospital; Brian Beacock; Joan Bland of Asquiths; Ian Pout of "Teddy Bears"; Sue Rixon of Nonsuch Soft Toys; Naomi Laight; Rosemary Volpp; Denise Naylor of the X-ray Department of Kingston Hospital, Kingston upon Thames, Surrey; Sister Marie Claire; Michael Morse; Heather Bischoff; Tracie Vallis; Felix C. Sear; Trevor Williamson; Bear & Friends, Brighton.

Special thanks to the curatorial staff of Bethnal Green Museum of Childhood for their support, and also to numerous family and friends, in particular Ruth Cornett, Kevin Edge, and especially Lynnet Wilson and "Cully" who started the ball rolling.

PICTURE CREDITS

Archiv/INTERFOTO 10, 12; Associated Press/Christie's 114; Bethnal Green Museum of Childhood 114; Camera Press 122, 123; Frank Spooner 122, 123; The Hulton-Deutsch Collection 12; © MPL 51; National Portrait Gallery, London 56; Popperfoto 35, 57, 71; Ian Pout 19; Rex Features 90; Smithsonian Institute 13; Sotheby's 6; Steiff Museum 12, 34; Topham Picture Library 56, 70, 91, 123; Ullstein Bilderdienst 34; Courtesy of the Trustees of the V&A 5, 10, 11, 13, 16, 17, 38, 39, 41, 59, 82, 89, 98, 99, 100, 101, 102, 104, 106; Paul & Rosemary Volpp 7, 119.

BRIDESHEAD REVISITED picture, Granada Television 119, reproduced with kind permission of Anthony Andrews and Jeremy Irons.

Special photography by Roland Kemp.
Additional photography by Pip Barnard, Jim Coit (in the USA), and Tim Ridley.

Watercolour illustrations by Pauline Baynes; black and white line drawings by Peter Serjeant.

Coloured line illustrations by Peggy Fortnum from PADDINGTON'S NOTEBOOK and PADDINGTON STORYBOOK by Michael Bond 86, 87. Reprinted by kind permission of Harper Collins Publishers Limited.

Line illustrations from WINNIE-THE-POOH © E.H. Shepard under the Berne Convention, in the United States © 1926 by E.P. Dutton & Co. Inc., © renewal 1954 by A.A. Milne. Colouring-in © 1970 by E.H. Shepard and Methuen & Co. Ltd., © 1973 by E.H. Shepard and Methuen Children's Books Ltd. 56, 57. Line illustration from THE HOUSE AT POOH CORNER © E.H. Shepard under the Berne Convention, in the United States © 1928 by E.P. Dutton & Co. Inc., © renewal 1956 by A.A. Milne. Colouring-in © 1974 by E.H. Shepard and Methuen Children's Books Ltd. 56. Reproduced by permission of Curtis Brown, London.

Rupert illustrations 50, 51 reproduced by kind permission of Express Newspapers plc.

USEFUL ADDRESSES

The Bear Museum
38 Dragon Street
Petersfield
Hampshire GU31 4JJ
Telephone 0730 65108

Bethnal Green Museum of Childhood
Cambridge Heath Road
London E2 9PA
Telephone 081 981 1711/6789

The London Toy and Model Museum
21/23 Craven Hill
London W2 3EN
Telephone 071 262 9450/7905

Merrythought's Shop and Museum
Dale End
Ironbridge
Telford
Shropshire TF8 7NJ
Telephone 0952 433029

Museum of Childhood
42 High Street
Edinburgh
Scotland EH1 1TG
Telephone 031 225 2424 ext. 6645

National Toy Museum
The Grange
The Green
Rottingdean
East Sussex BN2 7HA
Telephone 0273 301004

Pollock's Toy Museum
1 Scala Street
London W1P 1LT
Telephone 071 636 3452

The Steiff Museum
Margarete Steiff GmbH
PO Box 1560
Alliin Strasse 2
D-7928
Giengen (Brenz)
West Germany
Telephone 010 49 7322 1311

The Teddy Bear Museum
19 Greenhill Street
Stratford-upon-Avon
Warwickshire CV37 6LF
Telephone 0789 293160

MAGAZINES

Hugglets Teddy Bear Magazine
Glenn Jackman
PO Box 290
Brighton BN2 1DR
Telephone 0273 697974

Teddy Bear Times
Ashdown Publishing
Shelley House
104 High Street
Steyning
West Sussex BN4 3RD
Telephone 0903 816111